The
HOLY SPIRIT
and the
DAILY EUCHARIST
Supreme Gifts
of the
HEART of JESUS

by *Bertrand de Margerie, S.J.*

International Institute of the Heart of Jesus

The Holy Spirit and the Daily Eucharist, Supreme Gifts of the Heart of Jesus by Bertrand de Margerie S.J. Copyright © 1976 by International Institute of the Heart of Jesus, 7700 West Blue Mound Road, Milwaukee, Wisconsin 53213. Originally published in *Christ for the World, The Heart of the Lamb: A Treatise on Christology*, translated by Malachy Carroll from *Le Christ pour le monde: Le Coeur de L'Agneau* (Paris: Beauchesne, 1971), and originally in Portuguese, *O Cristo paro o Mundo* (Sao Paulo: Herder, 1971). English edition published and copyright © 1973 by Franciscan Herald Press, 1434 West 51st St., Chicago, Illinois 60609.

Library of Congress Cataloging in Publication Data

Margeries, Bertrand de.
    The Holy Spirit and the daily eucharist, supreme gifts of the heart of Jesus.

    Translation of capitulos 14-16 of Cristo para o mundo.
    Includes bibliographical references and index.
    1. Jesus Christ—Person and offices. I. Title.
BT202.M3313   1976   232   76-26708
ISBN 0-8199-0622-0

This book, the sixth in a series on the Heart of Jesus is published by the International Institute of the Heart of Jesus, Inc. Milwaukee (U.S.A.) and Rome.

This is IIHJ Publication No. 6E

Nihil Obstat:
    Daniel L. Flaherty S.J.
        Provincial, Chicago Province
        of the Society of Jesus

Imprimatur:
    Msgr. Richard A. Rosemeyer, J.C.D.
        Vicar General, Archdiocese of Chicago

January 16, 1974

"'The Nihil Obstat and the Imprimatur are official declarations that a book or pamphlet is free of doctrinal and moral error. No implication is contained therein that those who have granted the Nihil Obstat and Imprimatur agree with the contents, opinions, or statements expressed."

MADE IN THE UNITED STATES OF AMERICA

CONTENTS

KEY TO ABBREVIATIONS

AA: Decree *Apostolicam Actuositatem* of Vatican II

AAS: *Acta Apostolicae Sedis*, Rome, 1919 *seq.*

AG: Decree *Ad Gentes* of Vatican II.

CD: Decree *Christus Dominus* of Vatican II.

DACL: *Dictionnaire d'Archéologie Chrétienne et de Liturgie*, Paris, 1924 *seq.*

DB: Denzinger-Bannwarth, *Enchiridion symbolorum*, Freiburg.

DBS: *Dictionnaire de la Bible, Supplément*, Paris, 1928 *seq.*

DC: *Documentation catholique*, Paris.

DH: Decree *Dignitatis Humanae* of Vatican II.

DS: Denzinger-Schönmetzer: *Enchiridion symbolorum*, Freiburg, 1963.

DSAM: *Dictionnaire de Spiritualité Ascétique et Mystique*, Paris, 1932.

DCT: *Dictionnaire de Théologie Catholique*, Paris, 1903 *seq.*

DV: Dogmatic constitution *Dei Verbum* of Vatican II.

GS: Pastoral constitution *Gaudium et Spes* of Vatican II.

LG: Dogmatic constitution *Lumen Gentium* of Vatican II.

NA: Decree *Nostra Aetate* of Vatican II.

vii

NRT: *Nouvelle Revue Théologique*, Louvain, 1879 *seq.*
OE: Decree *Orientalium Ecclesiarum* of Vatican II.
OT: Decree *Optatam Totius* of Vatican II.
PC: Decree *Perfectae Caritatis* of Vatican II.
PG or MG: *Patrologia Graeca* (J. P. Migne), Paris, 1857-1866.
PL or ML: *Patrologia Latina* (J. P. Migne), Paris, 1878-1890.
PO: Decree *Presbyterorum Ordinis* of Vatican II.
PP: Encyclical *Populorum Progressio* of Paul VI (1967).
PT: Encyclical *Pacem in Terris* of John XXIII.
SC: Constitution *Sacrosanctum Concilium* of Vatican II (1963).
UR: Decree *Unitatis Redintegratio* of Vatican II.

TRANSLATOR'S NOTE

For most of the Vatican II documents used in this book, the translation is that given in *The Documents of Vatican II*, General Editor: Walter M. Abbott S.J. (America Press and Geoffrey Chapman, 1966). Acknowledgement is made as *Abbott*. Other papal documents and encyclicals, where an English translation is available, are quoted from those published by the Catholic Truth Society of England.

I wish to thank my colleague, Rev. Michael Downey, PH.L., S.T.L., of the Department of Divinity, University of London Institute of Education, Coloma College, West Wickham, Kent, England, who acted as theological adviser throughout this translation.

                                            Malachy Carroll

DAILY COMMUNION WITH
THE EUCHARISTIC HEART OF JESUS

PREFACE
THE PRINCIPAL THESIS
IN "CHRIST FOR THE WORLD"

When Christ for the World book first appeared in French (Beauchesne: 1971), it was extensively reviewed, all the reviews being substantially favorable.[1] This has encouraged me, with a view to assisting the reader to its better understanding, to write a special preface for this translation. In it, I summarize the essential theses which the work seeks to present and develop, theses which I believe to be at least in part original. I then go on to indicate the problems which it opens up, and which, as far as I know, are scarcely dealt with anywhere else.

Clearly, the basic thesis of the book is set out in Chapter XI. It concerns the universal co-redemptive mission of the human person, within a Church redeemed and co-redemptive, in union with the Eucharistic Heart of Jesus and with a view to the trans-secularization of the world. Every human person has the ability and the splendid vocation to transform and to make fruitful, for all mankind of every period, his trials and his death, by offering them to God, with and through Christ, in the Eucharist, for the salvation of mankind in time and in eternity. Consequently, the Incarnation of the Son of God becomes, in every sense of the world, an *In-humanation*.[2] Through his activity, each and every man can reach out, not just to a limited group (as Cardinal Journet seems to think[3]), but also to the utmost recesses of the human past and to the utmost limits of the human future.

This supplies the solution to the dilemma of Feuerbach and of many of the moderns: either God or man.[4] Already at the natural level,[5] each created person aspires in an obscure way to know and to embrace, within the whole of reality, all other created persons, seen and loved in God; and, to a greater extent, this is initially divinized by the supernatural co-redemptive vocation. The Scriptures direct our attention to this idea: for instance, there are the Deutero-Isaiah and the "corporate personality," the "good thief," and Simon of Cyrene, all symbolic of the destiny of everyman.

This basic thesis is expressed as follows in Christ for the World: "The supernatural activity of each human person reaches out to the extreme limits of space and time. Each person is, in Christ, with Him, through Him, and for Him, an agent of the sacred and universal history of the human race".

The other theses prepare the way for, deploy, and complete this basic thesis of a universal Christian personalism. They can be listed as follows:

1. In honoring and adoring the *Eucharistic Heart of Jesus*, the Church expresses her love for the twofold act of love, eternal and historically past, by which our Redeemer has instituted the Sacrifice and the Sacrament of the Eucharist; and for the twofold act of love—eternal and present, uncreated and divine, but also created, voluntary, and sensible—which leads Him to immolate Himself now and perpetually, through His priests and for our salvation, to the Father, to remain constantly with us in our tabernacles, and to unite Himself physically with each of the baptized in Communion, so that here and now, in us and through us, He may love all men with a sacrificial love.

2. Christ, author and perfecter of the liberating development, is the Prophet of the growth of mankind, their Priest and their Victim, their Recapitulator. *The Eucharist is the sacrifice of the development:* in It, Christ offers His life to the Father for the supernatural success of the whole human process at whose head He his placed Himself. He constantly redeems His Church to the point of making her the co-redemptrix of the growth of the world; consequently, the whole human universe, even at the natural level, benefits from the bloody sacrifice of the Redeemer.

3. Through Communion, Christ effects the temporal and salvific involvement of the Christian. The Eucharist, sacrament of perseverance in fraternal love and in involvement in the service of the temporal development of others, reveals itself as the efficacious sign of the very goal of human growth—the glorious resurrection (Jn. 6, 54). The Eucharist takes on, therefore, the character of *the sacrament of integral human development.* As such, it emerges as being the purpose itself of the In-humanation of the Word. Through the Eucharist, Christ "trans-secularizes" Christians—i.e. He causes them to pass from this world, with Him, to the Father, in the very act through which these Christians commit themselves to live, not for themselves, but for others and for Him-in-the-others.

4. Christ not only offers to all His disciples, but positively gives to them the supreme "evangelical counsel" of daily Communion when He, who is Himself the Bread of eternal life, makes them ask the Father in His name: "Give us this day our daily bread." The existential choice in favor of the daily breaking of the Eucharistic Bread leads, through the special grace of this sacrament, to the perfection of abnegation, and consequently promotes that self-relinquishment which conditions both personal and social development. That is why, if it is to be fully and supernaturally efficacious, the existential decision to work for the development of all mankind takes the form of a decision to receive Communion daily, when this is

practicable. The decision concerning development and the decision concerning daily Communion, therefore, involve one another. The daily breaking of the Bread of Life affects the whole Christian personality, as its most powerful means of psychological, social, and onto-logical integration.

5. The decision concerning sacramental and daily participation in the redemptive death of Christ may be regarded as an "existential major-decision" which will give meaning and supernatural and eternal efficacy to all the "minor-decisions" taken in the service of human development. It is a decision to offer up one's personal death, a decision reached in inseparable union with the sacrifice of Christ on the Cross as renewed in the Eucharist. *The existential major-decision concerning daily Communion modulates, therefore, into the existential decision par excellence concerning the co-redemptive oblation of the death to come,* a decision whose ultimate renewal in the final meritorious act of the free will recapitulates all the previous existential decisions and seals them with a definitive seal by conferring on them a meaning which is henceforth immutable, thus constituting the *supreme existential decision.* "The supernatural activity of each human person reaches out to the extreme limits of space and of time. Each person is, in Christ, with Him, through Him, and for Him, an agent of the sacred and universal history of the human race".

6. Coinciding with the sacrificial death of the last predestined, the Parousia of Jesus will manifest the universal action of His human free will. As instrument of His divine free will, it will transform, "according to the operation whereby also he is able to subdue all things unto himself" (Phil., 3, 21), the whole cosmos in order to make it the abode of the glorified bodies raised up simultaneously with the Parousia. Thus the Parousia will communicate the divine Goodness to the material world, for the benefit of the predestined; *the universe will become the priestly and inseparable garment of the divine Word made human*

priest. Far from being a universalizing of the Eucharistic transubstantiation, the parousiac transfiguration will coincide with its definitive disappearance, because it constitutes the end in every sense of this word.

7. Through man's work and for his survival, a *part* of the universe has become the bread of his mortal life; then, through the painful work of the Man-God in His Passion and through the words of His emissaries it has become His Body and Blood, the Bread and the Drink of eternal life, in order finally that this *whole* humanized universe, the priestly garment of the incarnate Word, will allow the eternal and immanent Sun of His divine Person to shine eternally through it in a ceaseless "diaphany." The whole universe, thus "trans-signified and trans-finalized" by the created free will and the created soul of the Word, will cease to be the food and the sustenance of a yet unperfected mankind, in order to become their transparent bond, their reward, their glorified extension in total submission to them, the new earth merited by the sacrifice and by the eating of the Eucharist.

8. The decision of the parousiac transformation will be, in the created will of Jesus, a decision taken in *the unique act of beatifying love* which results from the unique act of the beatific vision in His human intelligence. By the *same and single* act of love through which, in the first instant of His conception in the womb of the Immaculate Virgin Mary, He embraced the salvific will of the Father and instituted the Eucharist at the Last Supper, the Man-Jesus will effect, through his parousiac decision, the transfiguration of a cosmos at last in full conformity with the image and the glory of man and of God, the consummation of the universe and of history. This unique act of beatifying love effected by the Man-Jesus has never passed away, and will never do so (363 and 367).

9. In adoring the Eucharistic Heart of Jesus, the Church loves not only the past and present sacrificial love of her Savior, which she proclaims until He comes, but also the twofold loving act of His glorious return,

an eternal divine act and a human and unique act, to come and already present, by which His glorified Heart, forever wounded with love, will subject and assimilate to Himself the entire physical universe, will raise up all hearts, and will manifest perfectly to all His predestined the inexhaustible incomprehensibility of His creative, sacrifical and rewardng love, received from the Father and having the Father's glory as its final purpose.

In loving this Eucharistic and Parousiac Heart, the Church loves the threefold love—sensible, voluntary, and divine—by which this Heart will gather into a consummated unit the universe and herself, in order to recapitulate them in offering them to the Father.

In presenting these theses, we have arranged them in a sequence more logical than that in which they appear in the book itself, where the context makes this or that expression more intelligible. No doubt, one or other or even several of these theses may be open to question.

NOTES TO PREFACE

1. I have since developed some of these themes in a brochure: *Le Coeur de l'Agneau de Dieu,* published by the Apostleship of Prayer, Gregorian University Press, Rome, 1972. The numbers used in this preface refer to the pages of the book itself.

2. As one exegete has pointed out, we could and should have cited in our Chapter Eleven, in support of its thesis on the co-redemptive Church, the words of Paul to the Corinthians: "Always bearing about in our body the mortification of Jesus, that the life also of Jesus may be made manifest in our bodies . . . So then death works in us; but life in you" (2 Cor. 4, 10-12).

3. See Chapter XI of Christ for the World, however, where we express our great admiration for the theological work of Cardinal Journet.

4. Cf. H. de Lubac S.J.: *Le drame de l'humanisme athée* Paris, 1944.

5. P. 262.

1

THE EUCHARISTIC HEART OF THE LORD:
SYNTHESIS AND CONSUMMATION OF
THE UNIVERSE OF HISTORY AND OF REVELATION

The great spiritual and religious need of our times is that of a broad synthetic vision of the Christian mystery. Such a vision must be developed within an existential context, in the indispensable light which emanates from love. It must arise from one central nucleus which serves to render intelligible all its co-ordinated rays of truth.

There are some non-Catholic, Christian theologians of our age who have attempted such a synthesis; but this cannot be said of any of the best known[1] theologians of the universal and Roman Church.[2] Excessive specialization partly explains, but does not justify, the flinching away from anything which might resemble a *Summa Theologica*. That partly contestable and contested outline sketched by Teilhard de Chardin, who was not a professional theologian, has been acclaimed, notably because of its power to synthesize.

It seems a matter of urgency to us to contribute, if only from afar through pointers and indicators, towards satisfying that basic desire of all who have been baptized in the blood of the Lamb: to recapitulate and unify all realities, as well as all revealed truths, in the pierced Heart of the crucified Christ, in order thus to present fully the mystery of the universal redemption. For the created mind seeks to interpret the universe only in order to transform and to perfect it; the created mind aspires through intellectual activity to take reality into itself, only in order then to express itself outwardly in a world which is capable of receiving its impress, and thus to attain to the face-to-face contemplation of Divine Being, of Divine Love, of Divine Energy which shines forth with its pure light as well as with the diffused light of created reality.

We should therefore like to demonstrate here how the Eucharistic Heart of the Lamb of God could offer to Catholic theology the best initial and completion stages for its systematization: (a) in what concerns the sacrament of the Incarnation and the sacraments of salvation and of grace; (b) in relation to the consummation of the redemption and of the universe; (c) finally, in relation to the Word, Son and Breather, Predestinator, and created[3] and predestined Creator.

A. Meaning of the Cult Rendered to the Eucharistic Heart of Jesus

Both Pius XI and Pius XII regarded the devotion offered to the Heart of Jesus as the "summary of the whole Christian religion," and therefore as "the rule of Christian perfection."[4] Pius XII has clearly shown how this devotion synthesizes all dogma and all morality: "(It) is the cult of the love with which God has loved us through Jesus, while at the same time it is the exercise of the love which we ourselves bear to God and to other men."[5]

In line with this, Vatican II, with splendid insistence, presents "the celebration of the Eucharistic Sacrifice" as "the root, the centre, and the summit of the whole life of the Christian community."[6] The Eucharist, adds the Council, "contains the Church's entire spiritual wealth"[7]; it is "the source and the apex of the whole work of preaching the gospel."[8] Reading these statements of Vatican II and of the earlier popes, the least that one can say is that the Church's magisterium implies that the Eucharistic Sacrifice, on the one hand, and the devotion to the Heart of Jesus, on the other, are both at the centre of the Christian's life and of the life of the Church itself. How could they fail, therefore, to be the radiating centre of their ideas? If the world and the Church have for *raison d'être* the Lord present in a glorious, though hidden, and supremely loving manner in the Eucharist; if the loving action of the Eucharistic Christ is the supreme *raison d'être* of the activity of the Church—then how can we fail to conclude that theological reflection should take as its departure point the Church as it here and now loves and acts in the Eucharist, and should develop a synthesis around this mystery of mysteries, by first placing properly the two poles of attraction indicated here, the Heart of Christ and His Eucharist?

It is still the magisterium which is guiding us in this attempt at a synthesis of two syntheses, when it advocates a "particular devotion to the Eucharistic Heart of Jesus."[9] and also specifies its object:

> We can properly grasp how strong was the love which urged Christ to give Himself to us as spiritual nourishment, only by honoring with a particular devotion the Eucharistic Heart of Jesus, the object of such devotion being to remind us—in the words of our predecessor of blessed memory, Leo XIII—of "the supreme act of love by which our Redeemer, pouring forth all the riches of His Heart, instituted the adorable Sacrament of the Eucharist in order to remain with us until the end of time."[10] And certainly the Eucharist, which He has drawn from the great love of His Heart, is no slight part of that Heart.[11]

The Church, in honoring[12] the Eucharistic Heart of Jesus, is seeking to adore, love, and praise the twofold act of love, uncreated and created, eternal and temporal, divine and human, by which the incarnate and humanized Word has decided to apply forever the fruits of His redemptive sacrifice by renewing it throughout the course of history; and has thus decided to incorporate mankind with Himself in a union much more intimate than that of the bride with the Spouse, in the power of His Spirit for the glory of His Father. Is it not in the institution of the Eucharist that the three inter-subordinated purposes of the redemptive Incarnation shine forth: the salvation of the world; the exaltation of the Son of Man who draws all things to Himself; the glory of the Father who recapitulates all things in His Beloved Son?

Notice, in effect, the purpose of the institution of the Eucharist according to Pius XII: "in order to remain with us until the end of time"—i.e. until the end of universal history. Why? Christ wills to remain with us precisely in order to save us by applying to us the merits of His Passion, by thus kindling our love for Him, and by being thereby enabled to offer us to His Father in Himself and through Himself. It is our love for the only Son which saves us by glorifying Him, and it is by manifesting to us the riches of His love in the Eucharist that He enables us to love Him and to glorify the Father, supreme source and ultimate object of this love.

If the terms used by Pius XII place special emphasis on the Real Presence, they also apply to the Eucharist as sacrifice and as sacrament, Mass and Communion. In the same encyclical, *Haurietis Aquas*, we also read: "The priesthood and the divine Eucharist are indeed gifts of the Sacred Heart of Jesus. In the Eucharist as sacrament, He gives Himself to men; in the Eucharist as sacrifice, He constantly immolates Himself from the rising of the sun to the going down thereof."[13]

One could maintain, therefore, that this encyclical germinally contains a definition of the object of the worship offered to the Eucharistic Heart of Jesus; a definition wider, in fact, than the one which it actually gives us. This object includes the sacrificial love by which Christ, the Lamb of God, constantly immolates Himself for sinful mankind in all the Masses throughout history: a love which, by renewing the oblation of Calvary, makes it present here and now. It is this very love that we adore in the Eucharistic Heart of the triumphant and ever immolated Lamb.

In this way, one's ideas join up with a still valid current of medieval mysticism, and through the latter, with an Augustinian current.

> Formerly, the devotion[14] placed a primary and almost exclusive stress on the relations of the Eucharist with the Heart of Jesus, envisaged in the very act of His sacrifice on Calvary. . . . The Eucharist was, so to speak, only the Blood of the Heart of Jesus which was shed upon the Cross and through which souls are purified and nourished. The mystery of Jesus considered simply in the Eucharist was not, of course, ignored; but there was a preference for adoring Him there in His precise function of the Victim who continues His sacrifice and who applies that sacrifice to souls.[15]

In the thirteenth century, the mystical writer Ubertino of Casale remarkably specified the relations between the Eucharist and the Sacred Heart within the framework of the Augustinian tradition:

> Every visible sacrifice is the sacrament, that is, the sacred sign, of an invisible sacrifice. Thus the ineffable sacrifice which Christ makes of Himself in the august mystery of our altars and on the altar of the Cross, is the sign of the invisible sacrifice which He continually makes of Himself in the immense temple of His Heart.[16]

The visible sacrifice of the Mass, a sign which represents and applies to us the sacrifice of the Cross now invisible but made visible on the altar, is also, in the light of the same Augustinian tradition, the visible and efficacious sign of the invisible and actual sacrifice of the humanity which consents to what Christ has offered in its name and which associates itself with that offering. During the celebration of the sacred mysteries, Christ offers Himself to the Father as Head of the Church and of humanity, in order to involve every human person in His act of offering. The Heart of Jesus, giver of the Eucharist, seeks to enclose within Itself all hearts that consecrate themselves to Him, in order to offer them, in union with Itself, to the Father.[17]

It seems to us, therefore, that, integrally considered, the object of the worship offered by the Church to the Eucharistic Heart of Jesus may be expressed as follows:

> The Church, in honoring and adoring the Eucharistic Heart of Jesus, loves the twofold act of love, eternal and historically past, by which our Redeemer instituted the Sacrifice and the Sacrament of the Eucharist, and the twofold act of love, eternal and actual, uncreated and divine, but also created, voluntary, and sensible,[18] which urges Him to immolate Himself, now and perpetually, by the hands of His priests, to the Father for our salvation, to remain ceaselessly among us in our tabernacles, and to unite Himself physically with each human person in Communion, in order here and now to love all men, in us and through us, with a sacrificial love.

This perspective offers many advantages. It stresses the existential and actual value of the worship offered to the Eucharistic Heart of the Redeemer. The historical aspect (without historicism) accented in the definition of Leo XIII and taken up by Pius XII, is retained but also amplified: it is not only the act of the loving institution of the Eucharist and the permanence of the Real Presence of the triple love of Christ among us, that one adores in this Eucharistic Heart, but also His actual self-offering and His holocaust of ever renewed love. One can thus more readily set in relief the sacramental and ecclesial realism of this devotion: all the dimensions[19] of the Eucharist are contemplated in a cult inseparable from the act of worship by which Christ Himself ceaselessly constructs, builds, and completes His Church by making it grow.[20] Thus the Church adores the vital and life-giving act of love which ceaselessly maintains it in existence and deploys it in space and in time.

To this "vertical" dimension, are joined the "horizontal" advantages of this presentation. If the Eucharistic Heart of Jesus signifies His union of love with each communicant, the worship which is offered to It promotes a ceaselessly increasing irradiation of the sacramental grace proper to the Eucharist: namely, the grace of the dynamic growth of the supernatural and sacrificial fraternal charity which It pours into the world, for the eternal salvation of souls and of bodies. In adoring Christ as sacramental victim, the communicant drinks, with the precious Blood, the ecstatic[21] love which flows from His ever open Heart. The Eucharistic Heart is the Heart of the Lamb who makes each communicant a coredeemer by enabling him to love his remotest neighbor, not only as he loves himself, but also to the extent of the self-sacrifice which characterizes authentic self-love.[22] Such love realizes perfectly the magnificent conclusion of the Epistle of Saint James: "whoever brings back a sinner from the error of his way will save his soul from death and will cover a multitude of sins" (5, 20).

Thus understood, the Eucharistic Heart of the still immolated Lamb is truly the Heart of the Whole Christ, the Heart in which all men of good will, by offering themselves with Him as victims, are consummated in unifying love, in union with the Father and among themselves, through His mediation.[23]

Is there any need to develop at length the Biblical merit of this presentation? It links up very closely with the Johannine vision of Revelation: "Saint John there saw the Lamb in the heavens, in glory, before the throne, the equal of God; 'standing, as though it had been slain'; not slaughtered, but living and bearing the noble scars of the wounds which have caused Its death."[24] (cf. Rev. 5, 6-14). The Lamb of whom

Revelation speaks 29 times is a victim, but "a victim living anew." The immolated paschal Lamb appears in the Johannine poem "as conqueror," and this expression so dear to Saint John signifies "the sovereignty of Christ who dominates history and the world, associated with God in the glorification of the elect."[25] The author of Revelation saw the redemptive Lamb adored in Heaven because of His sacrifice, and giving a participation in His glory to all those who have profited by His Blood for the expiation of their sins.[26]

The integral object of the worship given to the Eucharistic Heart of the Lamb (such as we envisage this object in what seems to us to be a legitimate development of the principles laid down by the magisterium), corresponds well to the double aspect, painful and glorious, of the Lamb of the Johannine Revelation, as well as to the two aspects (death and resurrection) of the paschal mystery.

This integral object seems to be partly implied in the primitive Christian iconography of the Heart of the Lamb: a lamp in the form of a lamb from which there flows an eternal spring of oil in order to bring light and health to men. And in order to signify that it is by the merits of His Passion that the Lamb spreads His gifts, He is represented with a cross on His breast, and with a dove, symbol of the Holy Spirit, hovering over His head. He is laid on an altar or is represented with His side open and bleeding; or again, standing on His throne, while His blood flows from five wounds, joins into one current, and falls into a chalice.[27]

If one seeks to compare the object of this ecclesial devotion to the Eucharistic Heart of Jesus with that of the devotion offered to the Sacred Heart or to the Holy Eucharist, (and such a comparison is as necessary as it is inevitable if we are to understand more clearly the meaning of the Church's attitudes), then the following must be said. On the one hand, "the worship given to the Eucharistic Heart of Jesus does not differ essentially from that given to the Sacred Heart. . . . It is merely that the devotion to the Eucharistic Heart singles out one of Its acts,"[28] namely, the act of love by which Christ institutes the Eucharist, and, we might add, celebrates it as principal minister by immolating Himself anew and by giving Himself in Communion. On the other hand, and in a parallel way, one could say that the worship given to the Eucharistic Heart has the same material object as the worship of the Eucharist, but isolates its formal object—namely, the act of love to which we have just alluded.[29] Together with a certain identity, therefore, there are real differences between these three devotions. They are differences which the Church itself took a long time to perceive clearly. It was through Benedict XV[30] that the individual and specific nature of the devotion to the Eucharistic Heart of Jesus then came to be recognized.

Since this Eucharistic Heart is "the source and the apex of the whole work of preaching the gospel," it is to be expected that It should also be the point of departure and the goal of a systematic theology. *Its point of departure:* could a theology that seeks its source and well spring in reality, find a higher and more acceptable reality than that of the Eucharistic Heart of the Lamb? Is not the theologian who receives Holy Communion, in immediate contact with his Redeemer? *Its goal:* if every course of reflection returns, in its conclusion, to its initial principles and to its basic intuition, will not the theologian, after having considered the data of Divine Revelation in the light of the Eucharistic love, be better able to understand its fullness and its richness? Will he not find that all the rays of Christian dogma converge into the sun of the Eucharist? And will he not be inclined toward this through the sacramental grace of his daily Communions, all of which from the very first are polarized by the last, capable of leading into the pre-beatifying vision of Him who is hidden under the sacramental species?

B. The Eucharistic Heart of Jesus: Synthesizing Symbol of the In-Humanation of the Word, of His Church, and of His Grace

As we have already had occasion to point out, the Incarnation is not only the assumption of an individual human nature; it is also, through this individual nature, an insertion into all humanity, and, in a sense, an assumption of the morally good being and activity of this humanity.

Maurice Blondel grasped very well this "twofold aspect: it is because our persons exist that He (Christ) is a genuine man; but our persons, our human awarenesses, exist only because, in their depths, they rely on and are enlightened by the divine Person of Jesus. There could have been no Man-God, had there been no men-men."[32] In the concrete plan of Providence, there could be no Incarnation which would not be an Inhumanation. Humanity is a condition of Christ, who is the *raison d'être* of the world. There could be no "Christicity" without essential (and not just accidental) relationship with humanity.[33]

The In-humanation of the Word is an entry into the human species. "The whole of human nature is taken on Itself by the Word . . . in order to be united with that nature by means of the individuality which is primary in the order of divinization and of union with God. The individual human nature assumed by God has for its own purpose that of all human nature."[34]

Is there anything so very new in all this? By no means. Saint Thomas Aquinas partly retained the neo-Platonic anthropology which had enabled the Fathers of the Church to develop this theme. Did he not say that "all men are parts and as it were members of human nature; by participation of the species (according to Porphyry) many men are one single man"?[35]

Through His In-humanation, the Word has therefore become neighbor to each one of us, writes Saint Hilary.[36] But it is Saint Cyril of Alexandria whose

superb expression of this mystery wins for him the
title, Doctor of the In-humanation of the Word. Vatican II cites the following text of his: "For we are
all in[37] Christ, and the common person of humanity[38] comes back to life in Him. That is why He is
also called the New Adam. . . . For He dwelt among us,
who by nature is the Son of God; and therefore in his
Spirit we cry out: Abba, Father! But the Word dwells
in all, in one temple, namely, that which He assumed
for us and from us, that having us all in himself, he
might, as Paul says, reconcile all in one body to the
Father."[39]

Now, it is this same Saint Cyril who has most clearly
shown how, through the Eucharist, the concrete union
of the Word with each human person is effected.
Through the Eucharist, he says, we become "con-
corporal" with the Incarnate Word. In other words,
it is in the Eucharistic Communion that the Incarnation becomes fully the In-humanation of the Word,
and it is through the Eucharist that He "took up the
world's history into Himself," [40] the history of each
human person.

But let us listen to the great Doctor of Alexandria
himself:

> To unite us, to merge us in unity with God
> and with one another—even though we are, by
> our souls and our bodies, separated into dis-
> tinct personalities—the only Son has invented
> a means born of His wisdom in accordance with
> the counsel of the Father.
>
> Through one single body, His own body, He
> blesses His faithful in the mystic communion,
> making them con-corporal with Him and with
> one another.
>
> Who now could separate, who could deprive
> of their physical union, those who have been
> joined together through unity in Christ, by
> means of His unique and blessed body? For if
> we all eat of one bread, we all form one and
> the same body (1 Cor. 10, 17). There can be
> no division in Christ (cf. 1 Cor. 1, 13). . . . All

united in the one Christ through His sacred
body, all receiving Him as one and indivisible in
our own bodies, We must regard our members
as belonging to Him rather than to us.[41]

The Incarnation finds, therefore, its *raison d'être*
in the Eucharist through which we are physically with
Christ and with one another, belonging to Christ rather
than to ourselves. He has taken an individual body
only in order through it to unite all the others, and
to dwell in them all through this unique body. Here
we have a mystery of unity which has its origin in a
mysterious love. Does not this unity manifest that
Christ, in giving Himself to us in the Eucharist and
in uniting us among ourselves through It, does so
through love? Does not the Eucharistic Heart of Jesus
unveil Itself through the sign of this unity, which reveals His love?

With all this in mind, one more readily understands
what Saint Bonaventure wrote eight centuries later:

> I shall say with David: I have found my heart
> to pray to God (Ps. 5, 8). Yes, I have found
> the heart of the king, my Lord, my brother and
> my friend, You excellent Jesus. And then shall
> I not pray? Oh, yes, I shall pray! For, I say it
> boldly, His heart is my heart also. . . . Since
> Christ is my head, must not what belongs to
> Him belong also to me? . . . The heart of my
> spiritual leader is truly my heart. It is indeed
> mine. Jesus and I have but one heart. And
> what is surprising about this? Had not the
> multitude of the believers themselves but one
> heart (Acts 4, 32)?[42]

With even greater reason it could be said that,
through the Eucharist, the Heart of Jesus is the vital
center of the Whole Christ. It is through the Eucharist that Christ enables the Church to be ever more
richly animated by His invisible and uncreated soul,
the Spirit of the Father and the Son; and it is through
the Eucharist, sacrament of the unity of this Church,[43]

that He unites the Church in the love which is His life.

The Christian life is essentially a life of love for the loving Father, in union with His beloved Son, under the breath of the Spirit of Love which pours this love into our hearts (Rm. 5, 5). It is also essentially a sacrificial love for all men. The Church is a community of love and a hierarchic communion of love[44] represented and realized by the "sacrament of the Eucharistic bread."[45] "He who eats my flesh and drinks my blood abides in me, and I in him" (Jn. 6, 56). "We who are many are one body, for we all partake of the one bread" (1 Cor. 10, 17). It is of this unique mystery,[46] which envelops us in divinizing love, that the Eucharistic Heart of Jesus is the symbol.

The Church, sacrament of salvation, primordial sacrament which gives us the other sacraments, was born of the sacrificial decision of Christ, the Lamb of God, who in a sense instituted the Church by the fact that He instituted the Eucharist and immolated Himself in this very institution. At the same time as the Church was born of the pierced Heart of the Lamb, it received from Him the order and the grace to immolate anew its Savior and to immolate itself with Him, as true Spouse of the Lamb. Thanks to the sacrament of Holy Orders, the sacrifice of the Spouse is united with the sacrifice of the Lamb even in celebrating that sacrifice. The love that institutes the Eucharist is the same that institutes the Church as a community of sacrificial life and as a hierarchic society directed by sacrificers whose bounden duty it is to offer themselves as victims of holocaust for the community.[47] It is this ever loving and oblative love which the Church adores in the Eucharistic Heart of the Lamb.

Born of that Heart, the Church preserves numerous links with It.

The Church is a past birth which in a sense renews itself at every Mass and at every moment, since the redemptive Love is the ever present source of its life-giving love.

But, unlike earthly births, this birth is not a separation: the Church remains in the ever open wound of the Heart of its Spouse, as a place of residence where its life grows to fullness. In ceaselessly eating the Flesh and drinking the Blood of its Spouse, the Church remains in Christ, and dwells ever more deeply in His Eucharistic Heart.

Born of Him, living in Him, the Church receives this Eucharistic Heart in order that, through It, the Church may exercise the activities of love which form the basic expression of its life.[48]

In the Church, sacrament of the love that saves, the Eucharistic Heart of Jesus beats with sacrificial and joyous love for the whole world and for His Father. It is the Church which is the mediatrix and the guardian of the ancient and new commandment of fraternal charity, whose efficacious sacramental symbol is the Blood of the Lamb. Faithful Bride, it ceaselessly drinks the Blood which springs from the Heart of its Spouse —the Blood of Love.

The Eucharistic Heart of Jesus is thus the whole Treasure and the whole spiritual riches of the Church.[49] For what the Church recommends to its members and children applies first and foremost to itself: it comes to know the strength of the love which urged and still urges Christ to give Himself for His Church, only by honoring with a special devotion the Eucharistic Heart of this divine Lamb. One may even say that the more the Church comes to appreciate this fact, the more will it express its devotion to the Eucharistic Heart, through which and with which it adores the Father.

In adoring the triple love of the Heart of the Lamb which celebrates and gives the Eucharist, the Church glorifies this same triple love inasmuch as it has instituted and celebrates all the other sacraments, whose end is the Eucharist.[50] It also adores His commandment of twofold sacrificial love of the Father and of its brethren, a commandment whose promulgation He has deliberately associated with the institution of the

Eucharist, sacrifice and sacrament. Finally, it adores
the fullness of graces, the pleroma of gifts of the Spirit
and of infused virtues which exist in the sacred humanity of the only begotten Son and of which He desires to make all His brethren participants, through
the Eucharistic Communion.[51]

In respectfully consuming[52] the Eucharistic Heart
of his Redeemer, the Christian knows, at least in an
obscure way, that he is collaborating with the Word
of Life and of Love to spread and to communicate His
In-humanation,[53] to construct His Church, to merit
for many men the outpouring of the graces and charisms of the Spirit. "The flesh eaten in the Eucharist
is for the Christian a sure testimony that it is for
him that Jesus Christ became a man, and for him
that He has suffered."[54] In the Eucharistic Communion Christ intimates to the Christian that what
Saint Paul said applies also to him: "It is no longer
I who live, but Christ who lives in me; and the life
I now live in the flesh I live by faith in the Son of
God, who loved me and gave himself for me" (Gal.
2, 20).

C. The Eucharistic Heart of Jesus:
Special Symbol of His Consummating Love

In celebrating for the last time the Pasch of His
ancient covenant and for the first time the Pasch of
His new and eternal covenant with the Church, Christ
said to His Apostles: "Do this in remembrance of me";
and Saint Paul commented on this command: "For as
often as you eat this bread and drink the cup, you
proclaim the Lord's death until he comes" (1 Cor. 11,
26).

You also announce, therefore, this coming, this return of Christ: the coming of Christ at the death of
each and every person, the coming of Christ at the
renewal of all things; the individual and collective
Parousia.

The Eucharistic sacrifice is therefore an immolative

and actual remembrance of a past Event and of a future Event, the Pasch of the Head which is prolonged into the Pasch of the members and of the whole universe.

The Eucharistic Heart of Jesus, great High Priest, while symbolizing the past institution and the present celebration of the invisible sacrifice of the Lamb of God, also signifies its human, ecclesial, and cosmic consummation at the Parousia, and announces that beyond all immolation there will be the indefectible oblation of the Whole Christ to the Father, when He submits Himself to Him "who put all things under him, that God may be everything to every one" (cf. 1 Cor. 11, 26, and 15, 24-28). As such, the Eucharistic Heart of Jesus is the symbol of eschatological love, an idea we shall consider more closely. What relationships exist between the Holy Eucharist, on the one hand, and final perseverance, Hell, Purgatory, Heaven, resurrection, and eschatological renewal of the cosmos, on the other.

First of all, the Eucharist is the sacrament of the signal grace of final perseverance in salvific love. No means is more efficacious for obtaining this preeminently free grace of a final act of the human will which is at once free, meritorious, and liberating: "He who eats my flesh and drinks my blood abides in me, and I in him" (Jn. 6, 56). Although Communion cannot merit such a grace absolutely and in strict justice, it can do so with a merit *de congruo;* and the communicant, intimately associated with the prayer of Christ within him, can obtain this perseverance through his persevering supplications. Christ wills to give Himself within time, only in order to give Himself in eternity. Frequent communion with the Eucharistic Heart of Jesus is a sign of perseverance and of predestination. The love of Christ for us within time is the sign of His eternal and merciful will to give us eternal life, and the Eucharistic Heart symbolizes this twofold and unique desire.

However, the Eucharistic Christ does not compel us

to cooperate with His will to save us. He does not impose His divinizing presence on those who obstinately reject His salvific love, but He unveils the eternal presence of an immanent and reprobating Judge. Through their consciences, He condemns them eternally, and ratifies their decision to be separated from Him, a decision signified by their explicit rejection of the Eucharist or of the fraternal love of which, even for non-Christians, the Eucharist is always the source. We cannot with impunity ignore the fact that Jesus has loved us even unto the Cross and the Eucharist, "to the end" (Jn. 14, 1). Eternal Hell is the sanction for despising the Eucharist. It is the "second death": "Truly, truly, I say to you, unless you eat the flesh of the Son of man and drink his blood, you have no life in you" (Jn. 6, 53). Shortly afterwards, Saint John adds: "After this many of his disciples drew back and no longer went about with him" (6, 66).

Twenty years later, Paul severely censured the Christians of Corinth for another abuse of the Eucharist—no longer that of ignoring It, but of receiving It when unworthy to do so. It is precisely because in receiving Communion they were announcing the death of the Lord and His return, that Paul wrote to them as follows:

> Whoever, therefore, eats the bread or drinks the cup of the Lord in an unworthy manner will be guilty of profaning the body and blood of the Lord. . . . For anyone who eats and drinks without discerning the body eats and drinks judgment upon himself. That is why many of you are weak and ill, and some have died. . . . If any one is hungry, let him eat at home, lest you come together to be condemned (1 Cor. 11, 17-34).

Far from being a Communion, to receive the Body of the Lord unworthily separates the soul from Christ in this life and merits an eternal separation. God is not mocked, nor can one mock the gift of His incarnate Son in the Eucharist without changing that gift into a condemnation. One cannot with impunity mock the love of the Eucharist Heart of Jesus, which also shows itself in His anger against and hatred of sin. It is precisely because He loves the Father that Jesus cannot but hate sin. The Heart of Christ, present in the Eucharist, symbolizes not only "His divine love" but also "the sensible emotions which accompany that love: desire, joy, sorrow, fear, and anger, according as His look, His words, and His attitudes express them."[55] The Heart of Christ is therefore the symbol of the reprobating anger of the Lamb (Rev. 19, 15; 6, 16; 14, 10), which is an anger of love.

But the Eucharistic Heart of Jesus, which intercedes on the altars and in the tabernacles of the world for the salvation of all men, is above all the symbol of this praying, supplicating, and purifying love which seeks to purify souls here on earth in order not to have to punish them eternally, or to "tread the wine press of the fury of the wrath of God the Almighty" (Rev. 19, 15). Rather than being the mediator of the Father's anger, He prefers to appease Him through His Eucharistic sacrifice, while purifying with His blood those who drink it. It is one of the effects special to the Eucharist to remit venial sins,[56] and even, consequently, to save the good communicant from purgatory.

All the liturgies of the many rites of the Universal Church contain prayers for the still not fully purified dead.[57] These prayers signify that Christ has died, and today continues to offer up His past death, for the liberation of the suffering Church of purgatory. Much more than did Judas Machabeus, the Eucharistic Heart of Jesus sees the "great grace laid up" for those "who had fallen asleep with godliness," and that is why He ceaselessly renews His expiatory sacrifice "for the dead, that they may be loosed from their sins" (cf. 2 Mach. 12, 45-46).

In venerating this Eucharistic Heart, the pilgrim Church adores Its loving expiation for the sins of the members of the Church suffering, and associates itself with this superabundant satisfaction. Can it not be said that charity towards the dead, concern to win for them and to apply to them the indulgences which reflect and express the painful indulgence of the crucified and agonizing Christ, is the sign of an authentic and supernatural love for the living? "But if any one has the world's goods and sees his brother in need, yet closes his heart against him, how does God's love abide in him?" (1 Jn. 3, 17). Who more urgently needs that help than the Christian who has died with imperfect love and is temporarily unable to enjoy the vision of Love? And how could God's love abide in those who, enjoying the riches and treasure of Christ and of the Church,[58] of the Mass and of Indulgences, nevertheless close their hearts to these paralytics of the spiritual order, by refusing to assist and to deliver them? And it is from Christ received in the Eucharist that the liberating love for the dead proceeds.

But, just as the Immaculate Conception of Mary results from a more sublime expression of the redemptive work of Christ, the same is true of the perfect love which saves from purgatory. Of Itself, the Eucharist frequently received is the sacrament, the efficacious sign, of the immediate entry of the dying Christian into the beatifying vision of the Risen Lord, because It is the sacrament of the fervor of love. From this love which fills the soul of the contemplator of the triune Love, there arises the natural and glorified desire for definitive reunion with the body of which the soul has been (painlessly) deprived. The Communion of the exiled (1 Cor. 5, 6) in the body of the Risen Lord, merits the spiritual vision of this glorious body, instrument of all resurrection, and then Its physical and eternal vision.

Does not this follow from the teaching of Jesus Himself in His discourse on the Bread of Life, and from that of Saint Paul to the Corinthians? "For as by a man came death, by a man has also come the resurrection of the dead" (1 Cor. 15, 21).[59] "He who eats my flesh and drinks my blood has eternal life, and I will raise him up on the last day" (Jn. 6, 54).

How can it be denied that the risen Christ will raise up all the just through love for them and for His Father, and even through a grateful and rewarding love for that love which on earth led them to be partakers of the Eucharist? The glorious resurrection of the just will be, therefore, a visible manifestation of the love (as perfectly shown as possible) which the created and human will of the Resurrected Christ bears to them, and of which the Heart is the parousiac symbol.

To this great manifestation of the human love of Christ, a love which is itself the always inseparable instrument of His divine love; to this glorious resurrection of the bodies of the just, will be added the "resurrection," or more exactly the transfiguration, of the cosmos, their reciprocal bond, through the powerful action of the human will of the Lord. Even now, as the Church teaches, Christ, "sitting at the right hand of the Father, is continually active in the world, leading men to the Church, and through her joining them more closely to Himself and making them partakers of His glorious life by nourishing them with His own body and blood."[60] The present action of the Eucharistic Heart of Jesus is essentially an ecclesial action. Its first effect is the Church, His mystical and social Body. It is in the Church and by the Church, through its sacramental economy, that the Eucharistic Heart of Jesus inaugurates and prepares the final and eschatological transformation of the universe. The world, whose creation is confirmed by Genesis, is a human, anthropocentric world: the consummation of the visible world basically presupposes, therefore, the redemption of man which Christ has effected and effects by His miracles and by His sacraments, the latter being all polarized by the primordial sacrament of the Church.

This "pilgrim Church, in her sacraments and institutions, which pertain to the present times, takes on the appearance of this passing world. She herself dwells among creatures who groan and travail in pain until now and await the revelation of the sons of God (cf.

Rom. 8, 19-22)."[61] The Church therefore shares in the present condition of the material creation, the latter being polarized by its perfect parousiac consummation which is inseparable from the resurrection of our bodies.

The great exercise of the transforming power of Christ will occur at His Parousia: "We await a Savior, the Lord Jesus Christ, who will change our lowly body to be like his glorious body, by the power which enables him even to subject all things to himself" (Phil. 3, 20-21).

Christ will not limit Himself, therefore, to resurrecting human bodies; He will also transform the material world, making it "a new earth" (2 Pet. 3, 13), precisely in order to adapt it to its new condition as a dwelling for the glorified bodies of the saints. "Since all physical things are in a sense made for man," writes Saint Thomas Aquinas, "it is fitting that at this moment the state of the whole material creation should also be changed, in order that it may be adapted to man's condition then. . . . Since men will be not only delivered from corruption but also clothed in glory, it is proper that the material creation should then also be invested with a certain splendor of glory. Hence it is written: 'Then I saw a new heaven and a new earth' (Rev. 21, 1)."[62]

It is true that no text of the New Testament explicitly attributes to the glorified Christ this transformation of the material world; but the resurrection of the dead (or even of one dead person) is a much greater wonder than the transformation of the whole material universe, and therefore it is reasonable to suppose that the latter is included in "the power which Christ has to raise up the dead and to subject all things to himself." It is a power which the omnipotent Christ will use at the same time as He raises up the dead.

What exactly is the nature of this power possessed by the Man-Jesus to perfect the universe, and to complete the redemption of the universe in that of man?

What can be said on this subject in the light of Catholic tradition?[63]

At the Parousia, the human and created soul of Jesus will reveal itself as being the efficient, instrumental cause of the consummation of the universe. It must be borne in mind that, in effect, the supreme source of all causality and of all efficiency is spiritual: it is the Wisdom of the divine Will. Likewise, in the created order, the highest principles of action are spiritual. The transformation of the universe will result, therefore, from the power, not proper but instrumental, of the human nature, and especially of the human free will of the Man-Jesus, inasmuch as this freedom is the instrument of the divine free will. At the Parousia, the purpose of the human free will of Jesus will be to express the divine Goodness to the material world, for the happiness of predestined mankind, at the very moment when He will glorify mankind by raising up the dead.

In what way is the ultimate transformation of the universe and of nature dependent on the human, immaterial free will of Jesus?

In this exercise of instrumental causality, the principal cause, i.e. the divine nature, unites the instrument —here the human will of Christ—with the effect sought: universal resurrection and transfiguration. (That a spiritual cause, even merely instrumental, can change and transform not only minds but also matter, emerges clearly in the light of the divine causality in general, and, more particularly, in the case of the influence which man's intelligence and will can exert on his physical activities). The divine will of the Incarnate Word will therefore move His human will, which is perfectly obedient to it,[64] by directing this created free will towards all the times and places manifested to the created soul of Christ in the beatifying vision of His own divine Person. Jesus, seeing as the Word His plan of creation and sharing in His human will the universal causality of His divine will, will reach by His created will—the instrument of His divinity—

to all creatures in order to complete them by developing all their potentialities.

It is this magnificent perspective of a universal transformative action of the human free will of Jesus that Saint Thomas Aquinas, developing the thought of Saint Paul (Eph. 1, 10), already sketched centuries ago:

> If we speak of the soul of Christ as it is the instrument of the Word united to Him, it had an instrumental power to effect all the miraculous transmutations ordainable to the end of the Incarnation, which is to re-establish all things that are in heaven and on earth. . . . All other beings are governed by the soul of Christ who is superior to all creatures.[65]

Saint Thomas, therefore, presents the recapitulation of all beings under their Head, Christ, as the purpose itself of His Incarnation, and at the same time the work of His human free will as instrument of the divine action.[66] The ultimate transformation of the universe, orientated to the perfect realization of the purpose of the recapitulative Incarnation, could not escape the powerful, but not omnipotent,[67] human will of the Word made man. Christ will appear as, in the most literal sense of the word, the Savior of the World, the Redeemer of the Universe, finally become an harmonious cosmos[68] to the point of being the priestly[69] garment of the divine Word made human priest. The creation, "subjected to futility" by the first Adam, will be "set free from its bondage to decay" through the created and glorious free will of the only Son of God; it will be made "like his glorious body" after having been like "our lowly body," by the power which this second Adam possesses to subject the whole universe to Himself in order then to subject Himself, at its head, to the Father (Rom. 8, 19-21; Phil. 3, 21; 1 Cor. 15, 27-28).[71] Chaos will at last be cosmos. The consecration of the world will be completed.

As can be seen, even without transposition in terms of Teilhardian *genèse*,[72] it was already possible to reflect deeply on the relations between the cosmos and the Word made flesh, by methodically using the principles laid down by Saint Thomas Aquinas.

Such an undertaking can even claim to have a particular merit: more than on the influence of the glorified body of the Word, it stresses that of His human free will and of His soul divinized by sanctifying grace.[73] It therefore highlights what is most specifically *human* in the cosmic influence of Christ. It presents the parousiac transformation of the physical universe as the divinizing redemption of that universe and as the culminating point of man's salvation by the Man-Jesus; or, if one may so express it,[74] of the salvation of free wills in "cosmic situation" by the loving free will of the Man-Jesus. From this viewpoint, it must be said that, in adoring the Heart of Jesus, the Church adores His love, His threefold love—affective, spiritual, and divine—for the whole physical universe destined to undergo a perfect eschatological humanization. Jesus loves this universe which He creates for men, His brethren; this universe through which He forms bodies destined to resurrection; this universe which He will transfigure in order to reward His brethren for sharing in His Passion.

It must also be stressed that the parousiac transfiguration will be effected at the very moment when the glorified Christ ceases forever to work the miracle of transubstantiation. In the full span of the Church's history on earth, between the Pasch of Christ and the cosmic Pasch, the universe will have been partly transubstantiated but only in order ultimately to become completely transfigured. Through the work of man and for his survival, a *part* of the universe becomes the bread of man[75] and of death[76]—*panis corporalis est panis mortis;* then, through the Passion of the Man-God and through the words of His priests, that bread becomes His body and blood, the Bread and Drink of eternal life; and all this occurs in order that finally the *whole* universe, linked with the glorious Humanity of the Word, may appear as His priestly garment, inseparable and distinct, through which will shine, in an unceasing "diaphany"[77] the eternal and immanent sun of His divine Person, exposing His whole universe to the effulgence of His sacred humanity. Far from being a universalization of the Eucharistic transubstantiation, the latter will come to its end, in both senses of the word "end"; for its purpose was to divinize mankind and not the cosmos as such, since it was *for man's sake* only that Christ came to save this cosmos. Thus the transfiguration of the cosmos will manifest forever the love of the Man-Jesus for His human brethren. It will be at once human and humanizing, divine and divinizing. The Parousia will gloriously proclaim that the cosmic pleroma belongs definitively to the Church, the Body of Christ; it will be the fullness of Christ, including in that fullness the cosmic pleroma.

But, though destined to end at the Parousia, this transubstantiation constitutes here and now the sign, the pledge, the loving promise of that Parousia: "Whenever you eat this bread and drink this cup, you proclaim the death of the Lord until he comes." You proclaim therefore the coming of Him who will declare: "Behold, I make all things new" (Rev. 21, 5). Jesus, whose humanity is now totally divinized by His Resurrection—it was during His earthly life the imperfectly divinized humanity of a God[78]—will raise up in Himself sky, earth, and world,[79] making "the first earth" pass away in order to give us "a new heaven and a new earth" (Rev. 21, 1), in the image of His glorified body. The Head of the Church will become in a visible manner the Head of the Universe.[80]

It can be truly said that the universe—thus incorporated with the Humanity of Christ, as an extension distinct from this Humanity but perfectly subjected to its effulgence and its action—will be completely trans-signified and trans-finalized[81] by the glorified soul of the Word; it will not be transubstantiated, for, unlike the essence of the transubstantiated bread and wine, it will preserve intact its nature, which will not disappear or be changed. The universe will thus cease to be the nourishment and support of a yet imperfect humanity, and will become the recompense and the glorification, as well as the transparent medium, for this same humanity fixed definitively in God. In the present state of the world, matter veils and divides; but matter as transfigured by the glorious Christ will perfectly unite men and reveal them to one another without in any way contributing to their survival. The elect will enjoy, as regards their own bodies and matter in general, a controlling freedom analogous to that of the Risen Christ.

In the created soul of Jesus, the decision of the parousiac transfiguration will be a decision taken in the one act of beatifying love which results from the one act of the beatific vision in His intelligence.[82] Christ will carry out the transformation of the universe by the same act through which, at the first instant of His conception in the virginal womb of Mary, He embraced the universal salvific will of the Father. That act will never pass away.

At the level of the free will which corresponds to that of infused knowledge, this unique act, the most perfect created imitation of and participation in the Pure Act which is the Word in His divine nature, does not preclude a number of successive decisions taken by the glorified humanity of Christ. However, the decision of the Parousia, when time passes into the "aevum" which will mark the end of history, will remain as unique as this passage, identical with the pasch of history itself.[83]

Through love, therefore, the parousiac decision of Christ will effect the consummation of the universe and of history. It will be the supreme event of "the history of the divine Word,"[84] offering to the Father, as testimony to His glory, His own property redeemed and enlightened by the Spirit of God. In the heart of beatifying love, this decision is identical with that of the institution of the Eucharist, even though its material object is distinct and complementary. They both

have their place in the one salvific will of Christ, as
consequences of His one act of beatific vision. The
parousiac decision of the transfiguration of a cosmos
at last fully in the image of man and for his glory,
will have been justly merited by all the participations
by Christians on earth in the Eucharist.[85] In adoring
the Eucharist Heart of Jesus, the Church adores His
loving oblative decision to renew the face of the earth
in order to present it to the Father[86] in an oblation
which will never end.

D. Eucharistic Heart and Predestinating Trinity

We can and should apply very specially to the Eucharistic Heart of Jesus, Priest of Mankind, only Son
and victim of the Father, what the Spirit of the Father
and of the Son teaches us through the Church's
magisterium: "The Heart of the Word incarnate is
the symbol . . . of the divine love which the Word has
in common with the Father and the Holy Spirit. The
devotion to the Sacred Heart . . . is certainly none
other than the devotion to the divine and human love
of the Word incarnate; and, even, none other than
the devotion to the love which the Father and the
Holy Spirit lavish on sinful men. In effect, as the
Angelic Doctor teaches, the love of the Three Divine
Persons is the principle of the Redemption. This love
flowed into the human will of Jesus Christ and penetrated His adorable Heart, animating it with that same
love to such an extent that He willed to shed His blood
in order to ransom us from the bondage of sin."[87]

Now, it is indeed through and in the mystery of the
Eucharist that, in a concrete and existential way, the
Father, the Son and Their Spirit increasingly give
Themselves to us. It is the Father who draws us to
eat the spiritualized flesh of His Son (Jn. 6, 41-45);
or rather, the Father, who is in the Son, enters into
us with Him when we receive the Bread of Life (Jn.
14, 10-11; 14, 23; 6, 51). Their Spirit, inseparable from
Them, gives Himself with Them to us (Jn. 14, 17).

Through the Eucharistic Communion, we receive the loving presence of the Three divine Guests who have taken possession of our soul—an increasing possession which, however, increasingly respects our human freedom.

In instituting the sacrifice and the sacrament of the Eucharist, Christ made them the sign *par excellence* of the love of the divine Persons for us. In renewing His sacrificial immolation at every Mass, through and for the Church, the Heart of the Redeemer shows us in an ever fresh manner that "the Father did not spare his own Son but gave Him up for us all" (Rom. 8, 32), and that this Son offered Himself as a victim of holocaust to the Father through the Spirit in order to fill us with the fire of this Spirit of Love (cf. Eph. 5, 2; Heb. 9, 14; Lk. 12, 49). The Heart of Jesus present in the Eucharist becomes, when considered in faith, the sign *par excellence* of the Trinitarian love which gives itself to the sinful world through the wound in the side of the Lamb.

The union which Christians effect when they receive the Body of Christ, and thus "eat one another" in fraternal love, is the clearest sign on earth of the union of love that exists among the divine Persons: "Because there is one bread, we who are many are one body, for we all partake of the one bread . . . that they may all be one; even as you, Father, are in me, and I in you, that they also may be one in us, so that the world may believe that you have sent me" ((1 Cor. 10, 17; Jn. 17, 21).

The Eucharist, efficacious sign of the union of the Church in love, is thus seen to be the sign which contains and gives the Trinity, the latter being its source. The dogma of the Eucharist implies that of the Trinity. How could we say what the Eucharistic Christ is, without saying what the Son is and what the Father and the Spirit are? The Eucharistic dogma is the Trinitarian dogma become truth-for-mankind, truth revealed to men in a life communicated to men.[88] In the Eucharist, the Trinity transcendent and imma-

nent to Itself, becomes the Trinity immanent to us
men—the Trinity in the economy of salvation.[89] It
is in and through the Eucharist that the Christian
can ceaselessly grow in the knowledge and possession
of the Trinity.

The Christ received in the Eucharist is the only
Son of the Father, the Son turned towards the loving
Father, towards the bosom of the Father (Jn. 1, 18—
Greek) and, with Him, the Breather who, in yielding
up the last breath of His human soul, has delivered
to us the uncreated Breath (cf. Jn. 19, 30) which proceeds eternally from Himself. In symbolizing the divine love of Christ the Redeemer for us, the Heart of
Jesus signifies also the reciprocal love of the divine
Persons which eternally conditions Their common love
for us, and in which we are already mysteriously included, despite our inescapable contingence, by the
unique love, creative and absolute, of the Three Persons. The Eucharist is the visible sign, the sacrament,
of the invisible extra-and-intra-trinitarian love of the
living God (although in a sense nothing is outside
the infinite and immense Trinity). This is what we
must attempt to show, if even in a sketchy way. It
can be said that the Heart of Jesus symbolizes immediately the divine and loving Person of the incarnate Word, and concomitantly the merciful love of
the Father and of the Spirit for the human race—or,
to put it more simply, the love of the redemptive Trinity for sinful humanity. But one can also and more
profoundly say that the Heart of Jesus symbolizes the
personal and eternal love of the only Son for His
Father, in as much as it is an answering love to the
eternal and personal love of the Father for His only
Son; and that from this answering love springs the
eternal link of the uncreated *dia*-logue, namely the
Spirit who is personal Love. In this connection, the
pierced Heart of the immolated Lamb is the immediate
symbol (and not merely by concomitance) of the triune
Love, of the intra-trinitarian Love which is inseparably
(in the sense already defined) extra-trinitarian.

There is nothing arbitrary in this way of putting the matter. In his encyclical, *Haurietis Aquas*, Pius XII wrote: "The Heart of the incarnate Word is rightly seen to be the sign and the principal symbol of this triple love with which the divine Redeemer ceaselessly loves the eternal Father and all mankind."[90] Now, the divine love of the Word for His Father— principle of His twofold human love, spiritual and affective—is a love which is truly personal and not an essential emanation. It is as Son that the Word loves His Father, with a love due to the Father at the same time as given by Him, due to the freely given love which the Father has for the Son; and it is from this reciprocal love—due in one case and freely given in the other—that the Spirit springs, the Spirit who is "the personal Love of the Father and of the Son."[91]

But this mystery of the triune Love symbolized by the Heart of Jesus is also the mystery of the creative Trinity. Pure Act, eternally triune, is creative Act, not necessarily, but eternally and freely. In God, the creative act is not distinguished, except notionally, from the pure and trinitarian Act with which it is really identical. In a mysterious way, created persons are eternally immanent in the mind and love of the uncreated and transcendent Persons.

The Son is the Word, the eternal and uncreated expression through whom the Father expresses to Himself the knowledge He has of His own lovableness and of that of the whole universe, personal and impersonal, created in His image. He is the Word of the Goodness of the Father and of all men destined to be His brethren. In seeing in His Word the transcendent and uncreated archetype of all creatures, their supreme model, the Father creates universal lovableness of the human and non-human world[92] for love of His own Goodness. In speaking Himself in His Word, the Father speaks all things and all persons, including mine. ("One God produced one world by reason of His love for Himself".)[93] The Father wills eternally in love[94] the only Son whom He engenders intellectually by an act of knowledge of His own essence which is Love. Although He does not engender the Word *by* love,[95] the Father lovingly wills and ineffably loves the Word in whom He expresses His lovableness.[96]

The eternal generation of the Son prolongs itself, in some sort, in His temporal mission.[97] The pierced Heart of Jesus, while symbolizing His redemptive mission through obedience even unto the death of the cross, also signifies, in a visible manner, His eternal generation as Word of Love (cf. Jn. 1, 1b and 4, 16) and His eternal relationship of loving oblation to the Father who engenders Him in love. The Son is *from* the Father *(a Patre)* but also *to* the Father *(ad Patrem)*. In engendering Him, the Father gives His Son to the world, and this Son fulfills His mission by giving Himself to His Father for the sake of the world. Sent as victim of expiation for our sins, He becomes our advocate with the Father's love (1 Jn. 2, 1-2; 4 10). The Heart of Jesus symbolizes the temporal mission of the Son, precisely because it also signifies the eternal generation and relationship from which that mission is inseparable. And both are present in the Eucharist: the Father engenders His Son in giving Him to us and in giving Himself with Him; the Son loves His Father in delivering Himself to us for love of Him, and in uniting us in His intratrinitarian unity. The dialogue of love which the Eucharist creates in the Church, shows itself as an extension of the eternal dialogue of the Logos with His Father in the Spirit.

(We do not discuss here the question of the Heart of Jesus as sign of the eternal procession and of the temporal mission of the Holy Spirit, since this will be dealt with in the next chapter).

The Eucharist carries to its culminating point the mission of the Son in as much as Jesus effects in His twofold nature the synthesis of Eternity and Time, of the uncreated divine generation and of the created world; for, in the Eucharistic Communion, are deployed not only the synthesis of the limited and limitless (as Saint Maximus the Confessor had already

seen in connection with the Incarnation),[98] but also
the synthesis which is, in the most literal sense of the
word, a symbiosis. In the sacramental Communion,
the union of the divine Persons is united as intimately
as possible with that communion of persons re-created
in Christ which is the Church. The Eucharist thus
realizes a communion of communions, whose one mediator is Christ Jesus. If already, in Christ, "human
sociability, essential to each individual person, subsists
in the transcendent sociability of the Word in the
Trinity,"[99] the Eucharist for its part ensures the divinization of purely human sociability by making it share
intimately in the sociability of the divine Persons.

The Eucharistic Heart of Jesus is the symbol of the
Trinity as loving us and ransoming us in and through
the Eucharist. In paying devotion to this Eucharistic
Heart of the immolated Lamb, the Church loves the
redemptive love of the Trinity for the Church, the
triune Love which is at the root of the institution of
the Eucharist, sacrifice and sacrament, by the Man-
Jesus: ". . . that they may be one even as we are one,
I in them and you in me, that they may become perfectly one, so that the world may know that you have
sent me and have loved them even as you have loved
me" (Jn. 17, 22-23). Was it not after having given
thanks to His Father, in the midst of another prayer,
that the Son of Man instituted the Eucharist? Did not
the decision to institute the Eucharist occur as a decision reached in prayer? Bearing this in mind, one
understands more readily that the love of the Three
Persons is the principle, not only of the Redemption,
but also of the Eucharist, sacrament of the superabundant and free Redemption. This love penetrates
the adorable Heart of Jesus, the human Heart of
the beloved Son, making Him will to renew constantly,
in an unbloody manner, the sacrifice which ransomed
us from the bondage of sin.[100] The act of supreme
love by which our Redeemer instituted the Eucharist
in order to remain with us until the end of the world,

was certainly a twofold act, divine and human, of love
for men; but it was entirely orientated and subordi-
nated to the love of His Father.[101] Christ instituted
the Eucharist in order to be able to love His Father
in His brethren and through His brethren: "As the
living Father sent me, and I live because of the Father,
so he who eats me will live because of me"—and therefore for the Father for whom I live (cf. Jn. 6, 57).[102]
It was in obedience to the salvific will of His Father,
in order to keep His commandment, and under the
breath of the Spirit who was urging Him to do so
(Mk. 1, 12), that Jesus instituted the Eucharist.

Those who, through the Eucharist, often communicate with the Father and the Son in allowing themselves
to be drawn by the Father towards the Son, thereby
show that they are the elect chosen "before the foundation of the world," to be "holy and blameless" before
God, in love (cf. Eph. 1, 4). Is not frequent Communion the sign, not infallible, it is true, but the sign
par excellence, of freely bestowed predestination in
Christ created Creator and predestined Predestinator?

For Saint Augustine, election signifies predestination,
that is, "foreknowledge and preparation of the divine
benefits by which those are freed who are set free."[104]
According to him, predestination in Christ is at once
personal and social.[105] His doctrine of predestination
is essentially Christological: as the Word, Christ is,
in union with the Father, the God who predestines; as
man, He is the Head of all His predestined members.
As God and only Son of God, Christ predestines and
cannot be predestined. But all who are predestined
are so in Him and with Him as man; through Him as
the only Son of God. The final explanation of the
Whole Christ is the love of the Father who predestines
Christ to be our Head; the Father predestines all who
are His, in and through His only Son. Christ is the
first of those who have been freely predestined. Centuries later, Saint Thomas Aquinas said more specifically that Christ is the cause of our predestination, in the sense that the latter must be effected

through Christ's help, and that it is one and the same divine will (identical with divine Being, with divine Love) that predestines both Christ and us.[106]

In receiving the Eucharist, we eat in love Him who is the light,[107] the exemplar and the cause of our predestination, as well as being its source and its ultimate end. By the fact that He gives Himself often to us, as Bread of eternal life, and that He associates us with His prayer as Mediator in order that we may persevere in love, Christ manifests, as much as possible, His eternal predestinating love and His efficacious will to give Himself to us beyond death. "He who eats my flesh and drinks my blood has eternal life, and I will raise him up at the last day."[108] This is a gift which will crown both the merit of eating the Eucharist and especially the absolutely free nature of the first grace which leads to it and of the last grace which causes the elect to abide in Christ forever.[109] Nay more, even the grace of Christ which has merited the Christian's first grace and last grace is itself rooted in the absolutely free gift of Himself to His own humanity, which the Word made at the first moment of His earthly existence. Christ, who has merited our salvation and carried out the divine design of predestination of the elect, was unable to merit either our predestination or His own, both originating in a single decision of the absolutely free love of the divine Word in relation to the Whole Christ.

The Eucharistic Heart of Jesus is therefore the earthly sign of the salvific omnipotence of merciful and also freely given Love: the earthly sign only, since the Eucharist will cease to exist at the general Resurrection, there being then no further need to nourish and sustain our decision to love and serve Christ. But the Heart of Christ, forever wounded and open, will not cease to exist.

Before returning to the latter point in the conclusion to this chapter, we must more precisely describe the relationship between the free character and the remunerative character of the divine love for men, notably in the mystery of the Eucharist.

On the one hand, as we have already said, the free nature of the grace, and especially the absolutely free nature of the grace initially received by Christ, is at the origin of all our merits, which grow to their fullness through our frequent reception of the Eucharist.

On the other hand, the meritorious act *par excellence* consists in this receiving of the Eucharist from the motive of pure love, without concerning ourselves primarily with the rewards for doing so. Such receiving deserves to be called a *free* human act, the answer to the perfectly free nature of the divine love for us. Just as God has loved us through pure generosity, and without the least need to do so, we in return love Him with a pure love when we are not induced "to honor God through personal self-interest concerning body or soul, the present life or eternal life, but to do so because of the Goodness of God in Himself."[110]

Such purity of love given freely to God who has freely loved us before any possibility of a return of love by us, shines forth most resplendently in the consecration of reparation to the Heart of Jesus and in the Eucharistic Communion, the latter being the Christian's supreme sharing in the consecration of reparation which this Heart offers to the Father. Through Communion, in us and through us Christ completes His consecration to His Father as the victim (of expiation and of reparation) sacrificed for our salvation. "And for their sake I consecrate myself, that they also may be consecrated in truth. . . . God sent his Son to be the expiation for our sins" (Jn. 17, 19; 1 Jn. 4, 19).

In the mystery of the Eucharist, sacrifice and sacrament, we see a fusion of "the great duties of the Catholic religion: love and expiation,"[111] and also of the aims of devotion to the Sacred Heart of Jesus: consecration and reparation.

The Johannine idea of "selfless love," to use Dom Warnach's expression,[112] shows in a remarkable way that the freely given love of the reparatory consecra-

tion, in the context of the Eucharistic mystery, is supremely meritorious.

Saint John's Gospel and the philosophy of personality illuminate one another. A person genuinely achieves
what is best in him, and does so in an integral way, only
through the giving of himself to other people. A person is loved in proportion to the success with which
he attains to this supreme value of the giving of self.
The free nature of his doing so "motivates"[113] his
love. This, according to Christ in Saint John's Gospel, is the "selfless motivation" of the love of the
Father and of the Son for us, and preeminently of the
love of the Father for the Son: "For this reason the
Father loves me, because I lay down my life, that I
may take it again; if a man loves me . . . my Father
will love him; the Father Himself loves you, because
you have loved me; he who loves me will be loved by
my Father, and I will love him and manifest myself
to him" (Jn. 10, 17; 14, 23; 16, 27; 14, 21).

In other words, it is the active response of the only
Son and of the adopted sons that the Father seeks
through His benevolent love. At first sight, it might
seem that the eternal and uncreated love of the Father
and of the Son for their creatures depends, as if
through the addition of a new dimension, on the love
of men for Them; or that the love of the Father for His
Son is partly conditioned by the return of love which
the sacred humanity of the only Son makes to His
Father.[114] In reality, as Saint Thomas Aquinas has
clearly shown in his commentaries on Saint John's
Gospel,[115] no one can merit by his good works the
uncreated and eternal love of God, a freely given love
which is indeed the source of all merit; but man, and
preeminently the Man-Jesus, can merit the effect of
the divine love, viz. glorification. Ordinary men can
merit growth in grace, but not the first grace or an
increase of the already infinite love of God for them.
We must therefore understand the Johannine texts
presented by Dom Warnach, as expressing Christ's
solemn affirmation concerning two points: the death

of the Son through love for the Father is a sign of
the ineffable love of the Father for the Son, because
the Son could not offer His life unless the Father willed
that He should do so; furthermore, Christ as man, in
dying for love of the Father, merited from the Father
the manifestation of the Father's love, which manifestation is the glorification of His body: "For this reason the Father loves me, because I lay down my life,
that I may take it again." This "taking again" manifests the love of the Father, who was the original source
of the gift and who now rewards it. In an analogous
way it can be said that, when we love the Son, the
Father loves us in the sense that He manifests to us
that, in the final analysis, our love for the Son comes
from the Father Himself, who is completely "ad Filium."
Has not Jesus also said: "In that day you will know
that I am in my Father, and you in me, and I in you"
(Jn. 14, 20)?

Through Saint Thomas, therefore, himself inspired
by the Augustinian tradition, we see that this "selfless motivation" of the Johannine agapé is none other
than the merit, through a love freely given in the first
instance, of its own growth. Only in this way is it
possible to reconcile the texts cited with another text
of the same Saint John: "In this is love, not that we
loved God but that He loved us and sent his son to
be the expiation for our sins" (1 Jn. 4, 10). Saint
Thomas Aquinas makes this point explicitly.[117]

It is equally true that God has willed from eternity
the free nature itself of the love for Himself which He
freely gives us, thus in a sense inserting us into the
reciprocity of the freely given love which exists between Him and His only Son. It is this free nature
of our love for Him that He wills to reward.

Now, such a dialectic of freely given love emerges
preeminently in the mystery of the Cross, which is renewed by the Eucharistic sacrifice. Has not Christ
instituted and does He not celebrate the Mass, as
principal Priest, precisely in order to show us the extent of His freely given love for the free nature of the

Father's love for Him and for the human race? In His flesh and in His blood, through the Mass, He has given us the strength and the means to love God with a pure and free love which does not seek earthly rewards thereby, and which is even resolved not to aspire primarily towards heavenly rewards—without, of course, committing the error of despising them.[118] From this viewpoint, the object of the worship which the Church pays to the Eucharistic Heart of Jesus must surely be His pure and freely given love for the Father and for men; and its fruit must be our sharing in this pure love, the sacramental grace proper to the Eucharist. A final point should be made: since Christ's sacrificial love which we honor in honoring His Eucharistic Heart, is a freely given gift of the Father, then, in the final analysis, the object of this devotion is the love of the Father for the Son and for the world: "For God so loved the world that he gave his only Son, that whoever believes in Him should not perish but have eternal life" (Jn. 3, 16).

One sees, therefore, that through the sheer internal consistency of Christian dogma, the worship paid to the Eucharistic Heart of Jesus blends into the worship due to the merciful love of the Trinity for sinful mankind. To the undeserved hatred which sin directs against the Father and the Son (cf. Jn. 15, 22-26), these two devotions make the answer of freely given love. Against the sinful but finite will of man, is opposed the infinite and omnipotent salvific will of the Father and of the Son, which is expressed in the Eucharist.

Within this one salvific will, infinitely simple and identical with the Pure Act which is the Trinity, one must distinguish—by a notional distinction which shows its effects in created reality—between God's *relative* love and His *absolute* love for His rational creatures.

In commenting on these words of Jesus: "He who loves me will be loved by my Father, and I will love him and manifest myself to him" (Jn. 14, 21), Saint Thomas Aquinas recognized that, as regards their created effects, one cannot simply regard, as one and the same, the love by which God wills a particular good to one creature (i.e. relative love) and the love by which He wills all good—or the absolute love which expresses itself as the giving of self without reservation.[119] Through this second love, the Father and the Son come to dwell in the soul which They make holy. This is a privileged love, whereas God loves all His creatures with a relative love: as Saint Thomas explicitly stresses, God loves in this way even the devils, since He gives them the relative benefits of life, intelligence, and existence *(ut vivant, et intelligant, et sint)*. Like the human damned, the angelical damned are loved by God with a love that is even merciful, in the sense that He does not punish them as much as they deserve.[120]

In the infinite simplicity of the trinitarian Love, the universal salvific will is identical, really identical, mysteriously identical, with the absolute predestinating will of a number of the elect—a number whose size is unknown but which does not coincide with the number of rational creatures.[121]

In dying to fulfill the salvific will of the Father in relation to all creatures, Christ has saved the predestined, while adoring the permissive will of His Father as regards the loss of the angelic and the human damned. This is an unfathomable mystery which causes the weak human reason to fear and tremble, but also and especially to hope. It is a mystery of love which is not really distinguishable from the mystery of the new and eternal Alliance between God and men, renewed at every Mass by the one Mediator. The predestined Predestinator adores in this mystery of love the predestinating will of the Father, the Father's merciful will, while fulfilling the part of it which belongs to Him. The Cross and the Mass are inseparable from the predestinating Love which gives itself in the Eucharist as a sign and pledge of eternal and absolute giving of God Himself to His predestined. The Eucharistic Heart of Jesus is the Heart of merciful predestinating love.

E. The Temporal and Eternal Manifestation of the Heart of the Lamb, Symbol of the Pleroma

In his encyclical, *Haurietis Aquas*, Pius XII explicitly presents the Heart of Jesus as the symbol of the Pleroma of which Saint Paul speaks in the Letters of the Captivity: " '(You have power) to know the love of Christ which surpasses knowledge, that you may be filled with all the fullness of God' (Eph. 4, 19). Of this fullness of God *containing all things* (italics ours), the Heart of Christ Jesus is indeed the most beautiful image: a fullness of mercy, proper to the New Testament, in which appear the goodness of God our Savior and His love for men."[(122)]

This is a highly significant text. In it, Pius XII emphasizes, not only that the Heart of Jesus is a symbol of the Fullness of God, but that it is the symbol *par excellence* of that Fullness. He identifies this fullness with the divine Mercy, but explicitly states that it contains all created realities, and this is in perfect accord with the various shades of the word "pleroma" in the Pauline Epistles, such as we have already considered them.[(123)] The pleroma of God contains the universe and the Church, the universe which is itself destined to an eschatological integration in the Church and whose ecclesial integration has, in a mysterious way, already begun in the sacraments. This universe and this Church are, in a sense, immanent in the infinite pleroma of the triune God, of the divinity which flows from the Father through the Son in the Spirit and gives itself to the world in the measure in which the later, despite its finitude and its sin, is capable of receiving it.

The magisterium presents, therefore, the Heart of Christ as the indirect symbol of the cosmic pleroma and of the ecclesial pleroma—of the cosmos and of the Church as they are in God and from God; but primarily as the symbol of the infinite mercy of the divine pleroma which is at the origin and the end of the cosmo-ecclesial pleroma.

In the same encyclical, Pius XII implies that the Heart of Christ is also the symbol of the fullness of the graces which are in the Word incarnate: he does so by citing[124] Jn. 1, 16: "And from his fullness we have all received, grace upon grace." He affirms this more explicitly in the words: "Placed in His Heart as in a casket of great price, our Savior carries immense treasures of merits, the fruits of His threefold triumph (over the devil, over sin, over death), and He distributes them generously to the redeemed human race. It is this consoling truth which Saint Paul expresses in the words: 'Therefore it is said, "When he ascended on high he led a host of captives, and he gave gifts to men." ' . . . He who descended is he who also ascended far above all the heavens, that he might fill all things (Eph. 4, 8-10)."

Pius XII places a very special emphasis, therefore, on the Heart of Jesus as symbol of the pleroma of the graces of the Man-God. This point, among others, differentiates between the ways in which Teilhard and Pius XII, in documents published almost at the same time, regarded the Heart of Jesus as symbol of the pleroma. We do not find so clear a formulation in Teilhard, though his idea is implied in what he writes.

With Teilhard, the accent is entirely placed on the cosmic and finite pleroma in process of pleromization under the action of Christ. With Pius XII, the accent is primarily on the infinite divine pleroma of the mercy of the Word, as in a sense containing within it, in its immensity, the finitude of the cosmo-ecclesial pleroma; and then on the mediating (rather than intermediary) pleroma of the graces which are in the sacred Humanity of the Word.

Of all these pleromas, the Heart of Jesus is the symbol and the bond. It directly and immediately symbolizes only the divine pleroma and the pleroma of graces; while it symbolizes in only an indirect and mediate way the cosmo-ecclesial pleroma—the cosmic pleroma which derives from the divine pleroma and the ecclesial pleroma which derives from the pleroma of graces. It symbolizes this cosmo-ecclesial pleroma as contained in the immensity of the pleroma of the divine nature, creative and redemptive of the universe and of the Church. It could be said that this Heart connotes them still more than it symbolizes them. After all, the Church is the pleroma *of Christ* (Eph. 1, 23).

The divine and infinite love of the Word of the divine Goodness fills the finite universe; the human love, spiritual and affective, of the incarnate Word fills the Church. In these distinct senses, the universe and the Church are contained in the Heart of the Word made flesh. Christ is less in the universe than the universe is in Christ. Even if one considers particularly the humanity of Christ, one can say that the universe is in the human and wounded Heart of the glorified Christ in as much as it is no longer the universe which acts upon this Heart—as in the case of the pre-paschal Christ—but this Heart which acts upon it, since It is the symbol of the voluntary and totally divinized affectivity of the Man-God, who reaches out to the whole universe by His powerful action, but remains entirely distinct from it.

In adoring the Eucharistic Heart of the incarnate Word, the Church therefore adores the past and constantly renewed historic act by which the infinite pleroma of His divine nature wills to fill with Himself and with His activity the cosmic and finite pleroma, making His ecclesial pleroma share in the fullness of His graces (Col. 2, 9; Eph. 4, 10; 1, 23; Jn. 1, 14b), in order, finally, that "the whole fullness of the deity" may dwell "bodily" in us (Col. 2, 9b).

Christ is therefore the pleroma that ceaselessly "pleromizes" His Church, and thus recapitulates the cosmos. The pleromization[126] of the Church occurs preeminently through the Eucharistic sacrifice. It is in offering itself as a holocaust in union with Christ, and in immolating itself, that the Church increasingly becomes the fullness of Christ, His pleroma. It is in the light of the Eucharist that we must understand this beautiful statement of Vatican II's *Dogmatic Consti-*

tution on the Church: "Christ fills the Church, which is His Body and His fullness, with His divine gifts (cf. Eph. 1, 22-23) so that she may grow and reach all with the fullness of God" (cf. Eph. 3, 19).

It is in the Eucharist that Christ, the Lamb of God, fulfills here on earth the promise which He linked with the institution and the first celebration of the Sacrifice of the New Alliance: "He who has my commandments and keeps them, he it is who loves me; and he who loves me will be loved by my Father, and I will love him and manifest myself to him" (Jn. 14, 21).

The Eucharist is the sacrament, that is, the visible sign, by which Christ manifests, and causes to be experienced, not only His affective love, but also His spiritual and supra-sensible love, human and divine, to him who eats His flesh and drinks His blood. The Eucharistic Heart of Jesus is the supreme visible sign of the fullness of merciful love which is in Christ.

This Eucharistic manifestation has been set in splendid relief by Saint Bonaventure and the authors of the Franciscan school.

For the Seraphic Doctor,[128] the Eucharist is the sacrament of mystical experience. In Communion, the well-disposed recipient perceives the benign nature of the divinity and this is the gift of wisdom in action. Through Eucharistic incorporation with Christ, he tastes the sweetness of the Savior, a sweetness exceeding that of honey. With the Lamb of the true Pasch, he passes from this world to eternal life: "He who eats my flesh and drinks my blood has eternal life" (Jn. 6, 54).

A little later, in the fourteenth century, Raoul de Biberach[129] deals magnificently with the threefold manifestation of Christ, the way to the Trinity: Christ Jesus manifested Himself in the Creation, in the Incarnation, in the Eucharist.

First of all, Christ manifests Himself (to eyes of faith) in the Creation. But the contemplation of the universe, even with faith, does not yield an experimental knowledge of God.[130]

Then the Lord manifests Himself in the Incarnation: even faith, however, does not give us this experimental knowledge, since the event is outside our experience.

Finally, Jesus manifests Himself in the Eucharist: the grace of experiencing Christ is the special gift of the Eucharist. In the Holy Sacrament, Christ is the way to the Trinity. It is this for man's senses (thanks to the sacramentality of the sacramental species which orientate towards divine things); for man's intelligence, since the Eucharistic mystery demands perfect faith; and for man's will, which in this sacrament reaches Christ through ardent love.

If this manifestation meets with no obstacle, it should normally lead the communicant to spiritual marriage with Christ, living and acting in the Eucharist to purify him, to enlighten him, and to transform him as completely as possible. For is not the Eucharist the sacrament of the mystic marriage with the immolated and triumphant Lamb?

Whatever may be the extent of Christ's manifestation of Himself to him who no longer forms but one body, one Heart, and one soul with Him, such manifestation remains enveloped in the obscurity of faith and lacks "the clear vision that belongs to the life to come."[131] Nay more, it serves to make more lively the desire for this perfect manifestation which will mark the beatific vision.

We have already shown in what sense the Eucharistic Heart of Jesus is a very special symbol of His consummating love. We must now show why it is that the Heart of the Redeemer will remain, even after the Parousia, the indefectible symbol of the incomprehensible pleroma of the divine mercy, even in the midst of the beatific vision.

At first sight, this statement may seem absurd. How could the eternally pierced Heart of the Lord preserve a symbolizing function in the context of face-to-face vision? Up to the resurrection of all hearts, the symbolism is readily acceptable. But afterwards? Let us recall what we have already said several times:

the Word of the divine Goodness, even seen face to face, will nevertheless remain eternally beyond our complete comprehension. It can never be known by us, even in the midst of the beatific vision, in the manner in which It knows Itself—i.e. exhaustively.

It can therefore be said that the wounded Heart of the Risen Lord will forever remain the natural and glorified symbol of the incomprehensibility of the creative, redemptive, and remunerative love of the only Son, of His Father, and of Their Spirit.

We must add that, even after the ending of the whole sacramental and Eucharistic economy of the earthly Church, this Heart of the Lamb will, in a real sense, be the Eucharistic Heart, the Heart whose love, having instituted the Eucharist, pledge of the spiritual and corporal happiness of all predestined human beings, will remain incomprehensibly transcendent to every created mind.

There will still be place in eternity and in the beatific vision for the most beautiful symbol ever to issue out of human history and finite time. The Heart of Jesus, His Eucharistic Heart, is an eschatological[132] symbol in every sense of the word: it indicates, promises, and contains an eternal love, and in eternity it will still indicate the ineffable incomprehensibility of this infinite love.

With the forever pierced side of the Lamb in one's mind, one understands how Saint Francis de Sales could write:

> In the glory of Heaven, after the motif of the divine goodness known and considered in itself, that of the death of the Savior will have the greatest power to delight beyond measure the blessed in God; in sign of which, at the transfiguration, which was a foretaste of glory, Moses and Elias spoke with him "of his decease which he was to accomplish in Jerusalem" (Lk. 9, 31).[133]

It is in the light of the lamp that "is the Lamb" (Rev. 21, 23), that the elect will see face to face how incomprehensible was and remains the love which the Father and the Son have shown to them in the darkness of their exile, and now manifests to them in blinding clarity. In returning to their first principle, they taste the eternal pleasure given to the Father and the Son by the death of Christ, ineffably signified by the wound in His side.[134] It is in the death of His beloved Son that the Father finds His whole pleasure.

The worship of the pierced Heart of Christ will never cease, therefore, either in the pilgrim Church or even in the Church triumphant.[135] After having adored in faith this sign of the merciful love of their Savior, the elect, seeing with the eyes of the bodies raised up by Him, the glorified wound in His side, will discover, with the illuminated eyes of the soul, the divine love of which they were the object and whose continuing incomprehensibility will be their ceaseless joy.

The whole universe will appear to them as the garment, radiant with light, of the transfigured and "transfiguring" Christ. This cosmic and priestly garment, "dazzling white" (cf. Lk. 9, 29; Mt. 17, 2), will be forever the new earth merited by the sacrifice and by the eating of the Eucharist. The keeping of the new commandment of love will have resulted in the renewal and transforming of the world, even of the physical world.[136]

We are now able, in concluding this chapter, to complete as follows the definition of the object of the worship paid by the Church to the Eucharistic Heart of Jesus:

> In adoring the Eucharistic Heart of Jesus, the Church loves the past and present sacrificial love of its Savior, which it announces until He comes; but it also loves the twofold act of love of His return in glory, an act eternal and to come, divine and human, by which His glorified Heart, forever wounded with love, will subject to Himself and assimilate to Himself the whole physical universe, will raise up all hearts, and will manifest perfectly to all His elect the in-

exhaustible incomprehensibility of His creative, sacrificial, and remunerative love received from the Father and having the Father's glory as its ultimate purpose.[137]

In loving this Eucharistic and "parousiac" Heart, the Church loves the threefold love—affective, voluntary, and divine—through which He will gather together in a consummated unity the universe and the Church in it, by recapitulating them for the glory of the Father.[138]

NOTES TO CHAPTER ONE

1. Neither K. Rahner nor Schillebeeckx. A less well-known theologian, Dom Charles Massabki O.S.B. has published a synthesis of Catholic theology, *Le Christ recontre de deux amours,* Paris, 1962. Among non-Catholics, one can instance the syntheses of Karl Barth *(Dogmatic)* and of Tillich *(Systematic Theology).* That of Barth remains, however, uncompleted.

2. An expression of Vatican I (DS, 3001; DB, 1782).

3. Cf. DS, 536 (DB, 285): "secundum quod Deus est creavit Mariam, secundum quod homo creatus est a Maria."

4. AAS, 48 (1956), 313; a point specifically made in pars. 69 and 73 of the encyclical *Haurietis Aquas:* "absolutissima, si usum et exercitationem spectes, professio christianae religionis."

5. *Ibid.,* par. 71.

6. CD, 30; PO, 6. Cf. Paul VI: "The Eucharist has a power of doctrinal synthesis. . . . The whole of the Revelation is concentrated at this point, the most mysterious and most luminous of our faith. . . . And existential synthesis: in the sacrament, every virtue finds its nourishment" (Discourse of 21 August, 1968).

7. PO, 5 (Abbott, p. 541).

8. PO, 5 (Abbott, p. 542).

9. "Peculiari modo Eucharistici Cordis Jesu cultum fovendo": cf. note 11.

10. Leo XIII, *Acta,* 22 (1903), 307 *seq.*

11. Pius XII, *Haurietis Aquas,* AAS, 48 (1956), 351, par. 82.

12. Benedict XV had granted a Mass of the Eucharistic Heart of Jesus "pro aliquibus locis," celebrated on the Thursday following the Feast of the Sacred Heart. See AAS, 13 (1921), 515. This Mass can no more be celebrated. On the history of the devotion to the Eucharistic Heart of Jesus, see: L. Rayez, A. de Bonhomme: art. "Eucharistique (Coeur)," DSAM, IV. 2 (1961), 1648-1653; D. Castelain: *De cultu eucharistici Cordis Jesu,* Paris, 1928; A. Hamon, *Histoire le da dévotion au Sacré-Coeur,* Paris, 1940, t. 5, pp. 247-254; R. Brouillard, art. "Coeur

Eucharistique de Jésus," *Catholicisme,* t. II, Paris, 1949. On the relations between Eucharist and Sacred Heart, see note 29, and L. Garriguet, *Eucharistie et Sacré-Coeur,* Paris, 1925, pp. 305-310.

13. Pius XII, *Haurietis Aquas,* par. 43.

14. That is: to the Eucharistic Heart of Jesus.

15. Hilaire de Barenton, *La dévotion au Sacré-Coeur,* Paris, 1944, pp. 229-230.

16. Ubertino of Casale, *Arbor vitae crucifixae,* cited by de Barenton, *op. cit.,* p. 230; 81-84.

17. Cf. this text of Saint Augustine, cited by PO, 2: ". . . the entire commonwealth of the redeemed . . . (should) be offered as a universal sacrifice to God through the High Priest who in His Passion offered His very Self for us that we might be the body of so exalted a Head" (Abbott, p. 536). Father de Montcheuil has rightly directed attention to the importance of this idea of the Mass as sacrament of the sacrifice of humanity, the visible sign of its invisible sacrifice.

18. Cf. *Haurietis Aquas,* par. 67.

19. That is to say, the Eucharist as sacrifice (Mass) and transitory sacrament (Communion) and permanent sacrament (Real Presence in the tabernacle).

20. LG, 17; UR, 15.

21. We mean: the supernatural love which inclines towards the total giving of the self to God through fraternal charity, in accordance with the teaching of 1 John; only thus can the intimate indwelling of the Three Divine Persons reveal itself (cf. 1 Jn. 3, 18. 23. 24; Jn. 14, 21-23). The passage to sacrifical exteriority conditions the return to the interiority of the transcendent God.

22. Cf. Saint Thomas Aquinas, *Summa Theologica,* II. II. 25. 4. 3; 25. 7.

23. We recall that the growth of the twofold love of God and of the neighbor is the proper fruit of the Eucharist, sacrament of the fervor of love.

24. Mangenot, *Dictionnaire de Théologie Catholique,* 1, 1 (1923), art. "Agneau."

25. Y. M. J. Congar, *Mystère du Temple,* Paris, 1958, p. 247.

26. Mangenot, cf. note 24. One could even say that, in Saint John's view, all the faithful participate here on earth in the sacrifice and in the glory of the immolated and triumphant Lamb: "Feed my lambs" (Jn. 21, 15; cf. Rev. 7, 17); they are all the lambs of whom the lamb is the supreme shepherd—the lambs of the Lamb.

27. Mangenot, cf. note 24. In 1891, the Holy Office expressed its disapproval of images which showed, in the midst of a host, a heart surmounted with flames, or hosts falling from the Heart of Jesus on to a paten: cf. Hamon, *op. cit.,* pp. 248-249. On the other hand, no objection could be made against

the images representing Jesus and His Heart burning with love for men, having before Him a chalice and bread: the Heart of Jesus instituting the Eucharist.

28. Hamon, *op. cit.*, p. 253. Besides, is it not to be expected that the very origin of the Christian liturgy should be the object of a liturgical celebration?

29. In 1949, Pius XII specified as follows the difference between devotion to the Sacred Heart and devotion to the Eucharist: "These two salvific devotions cannot be confused as to their object, or their motive, or their end, or their origin. . . . One honors the love of the Lord under the natural symbol of His Heart; the other adores this flesh and this blood in which this love is entirely given to us" (AAS, 41 (1949, 331). It could be said that the devotion to the Eucharistic Heart of Jesus isolates, in the devotion to the Heart of Jesus, one of His acts; and, in the Eucharistic devotion, its formal object. These devotions are not, therefore, purely and simply identical with one another.

30. Benedict XV promoted the devotion to the Eucharistic Heart of Jesus throughout his whole reign (see Castelain and Hamon, *op. cit.*, pp. 251-252). He declared: "I shall myself propagate this devotion. . . . It is the jewel of the devotion to the Sacred Heart. . . . The devotion to the Eucharistic Heart will be a source of graces for souls; *it will spread more and more in the Church (ibid., p. 252)."* There is a prophetic accent in this declaration, and it is our fervent wish that the present book may in some way contribute to the realization of this prophecy.

31. Cf. the teaching of God the Father to Saint Catherine of Siena, *Dialogue* XIII (43): "The just who have lived in charity and who die in love . . . see the happiness which I have prepared for them. . . . They thus taste eternal life before they have left their mortal remains, before the soul is separated from the body." The perfect taste their destined beatitude even before leaving the body at the moment of death, whereas the imperfect enter into purgatory.

32. Cited by R. Marlé S.J., *Au coeur de la crise moderniste,* Paris, 1960, p. 240.

33. Cf. G. Martelet S.J., in *Problèmes actuels de Christologie,* Paris, 1965, p. 42.

34. M. J. Nicolas O.P., *ibid,* p 82 It will be noted that the author expresses an idea which is in line with Greek patristic thought as taken up by Saint Thomas Aquinas; he does not say that all human persons are seized by the Word. Human persons having been corrupted by original sin only because of nature, Christ first repairs this nature in order fully to repair the human persons at the glorious Resurrection; cf. the following note.

35. Saint Thomas Aquinas, In Romanos 5, lectio III, par.

410: Marietti, Rome, 1953. It is in the context of original sin that the text cited here occurs.

36. Saint Hilary on Mt. 19, 5: Christus "omnium nostrum corpus assumpsit et unicuique nostrum assumpti corporis ratione factus est proximus" (PL, 9, 1025).

37. Saint Cyril of Alexandria, author of this text, in thus interpreting Jn. 1, 14 (Mersch translates as *en* rather than the customary *parmi*) highlights that it should be interpreted in conjunction with Jn. 17, 21, 23. In the prologue, it is probable that John already intended to allude to the immanence of Christ *in* us through grace and the Eucharist. It is especially important to compare this use of the preposition *in* with numerous analogues of Jn. 15: allegory of the Vine.

38. On this Platonic view and on the unity of the human species, see L. Malevez S.J., "l'Eglise dans le Christ," *Recherches de Science Religieuse,* 25 (1935), pp. 260 and 418; R. Arnou S.J., art. "Platonisme des Pères," *Dictionnaire de Théologie catholique,* XII, 2347 (1935).

39. Saint Cyril of Alexandria, *in Jn.* 1, 14 (PG, 73, 161-164) cited by Mersch, *op. cit.,* vol. I, pp. 516-517, Paris, 1951; and by AG, 7. 3.

40. GS, 38. 1.

41. Saint Cyril of Alexandria, *in Jn.* 11, 11 (PG, 74, 560): cited by Mersch, *op. cit.,* p. 505. Cyril explicitly refers to Eph. 3, 6 where Paul speaks of nations "con-corporal" (sussôma) as sharing the promise of God in Christ. The term in Pauline, not coined by Cyril, who eloquently adds: "If we are all concorporal one with another *in Christ,* and not just one with another but also with Him who comes *in* us through his flesh, how could we not all be one, and one in one another, and in Christ?"

42. Saint Bonaventure, *Vitis Mystica,* chap. III.

43. Saint Thomas Aquinas, *Summa Theologica,* III. 73. 2, *sed contra;* III. 73. 3; III. 80. 4 and 5. 2.

44. LG, 8 (communitas) and 9 (communio).

45. LG, 3.

46. Cf. NA, 1: ". . . that ultimate and unutterable mystery which engulfs our being, and whence we take our rise, and whither our journey leads us" (Abbott, p. 661).

47. Cf. DS, 1739-1741 (DB, 938); DS, 3847; LG, 11. 1.

48. We are drawing here on G. de Broglie S.J.: *Le Sacré-Coeur et la doctrine du Corps Mystique* (Apostolat de la prière, Toulouse, 1946); and on certain patristic texts, notably of Saint Ambrose: "cubiculum Ecclesiae corpus est Christi" (*in Ps.* 118, sermo I, par. 16; PL, 15, 1271; the text is an allusion to Mt. 6, 6: the wounds of Christ constitute the room into which one must retire to pray to the Father in secret); and on Saint Jerome: "De Christo et Ecclesia omnis credentium multitudo generata est. Quae unum Ecclesiae corpus effecta, rursum in latere Christi ponitur, et costae locum replet,

et unum viri corpus efficitur" (*in Eph.* 5, 31; PL, 26, 569).

49. PO, 5. 2 (citing Saint Thomas Aquinas, *Summa Theologica,* III. 65. 3. 1; 79. 1).

50. PO, 5. 2: "sacramenta, sicut et omnia ecclesiastica ministeria et opera apostolatus, cum Sacra Eucharistica cohaerent et ad eam ordinantur."

51. Cf. Jn. 1, 16; Pius XII, *Myst. Corp.,* par. 47; in this pleroma adored by the Church, there also figured the *actual* graces received by Christ or transmitted by Him inasmuch as they are all identical with Pure Act, with God who is Love and Light (1 Jn. 4, 16; 1. 5). All this is also implied in the worship rendered by the Church to the Eucharistic Heart of Jesus.

52. Cf. the original meaning of the Greek verb, *trôgôn,* used in Jn. 6, 54.

53. An allusion to Bossuet's famous definition of the Church: "le Christ répandu et communiqué."

54. Bossuet, *Méditations sur l'Evangile,* part 1, la Cène, 48th day.

55. Pius XII, *Haurietis Aquas,* par. 32, AAS, 48 (1956), 327. The Pope here cites this text of Saint Thomas Aquinas (*Summa Theologica,* I. II. 48. 4) which he applies to Christ: "the turmoil of anger spreads to the exterior of the body, especially to those parts where the influence of the heart is most powerfully felt, as the eyes, the face, the tongue." The cult of the Sacred Heart signifies for the Church, therefore, the cult of the holy anger of Christ: cf. Jn. 2, 15 *seq.;* Mk. 3, 5. One sees how free the Church is from the sentimentalities sometimes attributed to it: cf. *Haurietis Aquas,* par. 38: "The Heart of Jesus trembled with a holy indignation" (Latin text, 330).

56. Cf. Saint Thomas Aquinas, *Summa Theologica,* III. 79. 4.

57. Our reference is to those who have not yet made full satisfaction to the loving and salvific justice of God, and have not paid all the temporal punishment due to their venial sins.

58. This treasury of the Church is Christ Himself, "in whom are abundantly the satisfactions and the merits of His redemption," as Paul VI says in the apostolic constitution *Indulgentiarum Dominus,* 11, par. 5, AAS, 59 (1967), 11-12. The text specifies in what sense the merits of the saints also form part of this treasury.

59. Paul, in fact, does not speak explicitly about the link between earthly Eucharist and glorious Resurrection. One can maintain, however, that he does so implicitly or negatively in I Cor. 11, 27, by leaving it to be inferred that unworthy Communion merits eternal damnation.

60. LG, 48. 2. It is clear that the worship paid by the Church to the Eucharist Heart of Jesus has also for its object the constant Eucharistic attraction exercised by the glorified Christ,

who ceaselessly wills to convert mankind.

61. LG, 48. 3 (Abbott, 79).

62. Saint Thomas Aquinas, *Summa con. Gen.*, IV. 97.

63. Here and in the following paragraphs, we are following the fine article by John H. Wright S.J., "The Consummation of the Universe in Christ," (*Gregorianum*, 39 1958), 285-294. We consider that this short article has made a very important contribution to the development of a "cosmic Christology."

64. Cf. the declarations of Constantinople III (681) on the complete divinization of the human will of Jesus, united with but distinct from His divine will: DS, 556 (DB, 291).

65. Saint Thomas Aquinas, *Summa Theologica*, 13. 2; 59. 6. 3. The soul of Christ has therefore the power to effect the transfiguration and even the miraculous transformations of the whole physical universe, in the measure in which such changes are orientated to the recapitulative purpose of the Incarnation.

66. Note that the recapitulation, even in its material aspect, is therefore the work of the created and immaterial free will of the Man-God.

67. Saint Thomas Aquinas (*Summa Theologica*, III. 13. 2) specifies that only God can create or annihilate, and this is something which the human soul of Christ could not do, even instrumentally.

68. Clearly, a world in the grip of "futility," and "decay" (Rm. 8, 20-21) is not yet a properly orientated and harmonious cosmos. The whole creation is "groaning in travail" to bring forth this cosmos in which the power of Christ will transform it.

69. Saint Thomas Aquinas clearly teaches that men have merited the glorification of the universe: "this glory, the irrational and insensible bodies have certainly not merited; but man has merited that it should be bestowed on the universe, inasmuch as this glory contributes to increase the glory of man. Thus someone could merit that decorations be placed on his coat, without the coat itself having merited them." (*Summa Theologica*, Supplement, III. 91. 1). The universe is therefore represented by Saint Thomas as man's garment. This is a very rich image, which implies that the universe is a garment fashioned by man. The universe is also presented as due to be glorified as a result of man's merits and for his glory. These merits are, of course, rooted in the merit of the Passion of Christ, The Priest of the cosmos. It is therefore correct to say that the final cosmos, succeeding to the initial chaos, will be the priestly garment of Christ, a garment completely dyed in His Blood.

70. Cf. Saint Augustine, *Enarr. in Ps.* 109, 4 (PL, 37, 1459): "as born of the Father, God with God, He is co-eternal with Him who engendered Him, He is not Priest; but He is Priest

because of the Victim whom He has received from us and whom He offers for us."

71. It will be noted that in these three Pauline texts, the same Greek verb is used: "hupotassein," meaning "to subject."

72. Cf. a Teilhard text referred to in our note 112 to Chapter Four of *Christ for the World*.

73. The theologians are unanimous in saying that Christ has been divinized, in His created soul, through sanctifying grace. Cf. Saint Thomas Aquinas, *Summa Theologica*, II. 7. 1. 1: "quia cum unitate personae remanet distinctio naturarum, anima Christi non est per suam essentiam divina. Unde oportet quod fiat divina per participationem, quae est secundum gratiam." This enables Father Fransen S.J. to observe very exactly: "Christ has divinized His own human nature in humanizing it"—i.e. in causing it to grow to its full and perfect development (*Problèmes de l'Autorité*, Paris, 1961, p. 62).

74. We mean that these free wills are not only limited, but that they are also conditioned by the interplay of secondary causes which constitute the whole of the created world.

75. Clearly, bread is not a substance in exactly the same way as we apply the word to natural things on which man has not worked. Bread is a substance whose existence as such depends on man's labor and whose purpose is to be man's food. In a more proximate and immediate way than do many other substances, it fulfills the purpose of the whole physical universe—i.e. to serve man. However, in transforming wheat into bread by his labor, man does not create the substance of bread (cf. J. de Finance S.J., *Connaissance de l'Etre*, Paris, 1966, pp. 250-285).

76. Cf. the commentary of Saint Thomas Aquinas on Jn. 6, 35: "I am the bread of life": "panis corporalis est panis mortis qui non competit nisi ad restaurandum defectum mortalitatis, unde et solum in hac vita mortali necessarius est. Non dat vitam set tantum praeexistentem sustentat ad tempus" (*Super Evang. S. Joannis lectura*, Marietti, Turin, 1952, par. 914.

77. One knows that Father Teilhard de Chardin regarded the universe as a "diaphany" or transparency of God. See *Milieu Divin*, p. 162: "Not Your Epiphany, Jesus, but Your diaphany."

78. Cf. Saint Ambrose: "Tunc secundum carnem homo, nunc per omnia Deus" (PL, 16, 1341).

79. Cf. Saint Ambrose: "Resurrexit in Eo mundus, resurrexit in Eo coelum, resurrexit in Eo terra" (PL, 16, 1354).

80. Cf. Col. 1, 18—and the commentary on it by Father Lamarche S.J. in *Le Christ vivant*, Paris, 1966, p. 70: "Is not Christ called both Head of the Church and Head of the universe? This use of the same word for both ideas shows quite properly the one and only saving action exerted by

Christ over the Church and the universe; but this identity
of verbal usage does not exclude real differences. It is in
a privileged manner that Christ is the Head of the Church,
since the Church alone is the part of the universe that becomes assimilated to Christ's body and which is given the
title, (Mystical) Body of Christ. Through its growth, the
Church is to take on the dimensions of the universe." It
is therefore in an imperfect manner only that the physical
universe forms part, here and now, of the Church; it will
be fully part of it at the Parousia.

81. We are referring here to the declarations of Paul VI
in the encyclical *Mysterium Fidei,* AAS, 57 (1965), 766:
"Peracta transsubstantiatione, species panis et vini novam pro-
cul dubio induunt significationem, novumque finem, cum am-
plius non sint communis panis et communis potus, sed signum
rei sanctae signumque spiritualis alimoniae; sed ideo novam
induunt significationem et novam finem, quia novam conti-
nent 'realitatem,' quam merito *ontologicam* dicimus." Cf. *ibid.,*
p. 755. At the Parousia, it will be not only the species of
bread and wine, but the whole universe, that will be "trans-
signified" and "trans-finalized" without preliminary transubstantiation.

82. Cf. Saint Thomas Aquinas, *Compendium Theol.,* I. 149.

83. On *aevum,* see Saint Thomas Aquinas, *Summa Theologica,* I. 10. 5. 1, 2; Michel A., DTC, V. 1 (1913), art. *"Eternité,"*
col. 912-921.

84. Pius XII, Christmas 1957, AAS, 50 (1958) 17. Cf. also
H. de Lubac S.J.: *La pensée religieuse du P. Teilhard de
Chardin,* Paris, 1962, pp. 185-200.

85. Thus, the human free will conditions, in the providen-
tial plan, not necessarily the hour of the Parousia, but the
existence itself of the cosmic consequences of this supreme
event, which is identical with the Second Coming of the Son
of Man. Communion with the Transfigurator merits the
cosmic Transfiguration.

86. The words "until he comes" (1 Cor. 11, 26) must be
read in the light of 15, 24-28, of the same Epistle: in order
to subject all things to the Father.

87. Pius XII, *Haurietis Aquas,* par. 33 and 54: AAS, 48
(1956), 327, 338.

88. Cf. Mersch S.J., *op. cit.,* t. II, p. 13. Cf. Jn. 6, 45-57

89. Cf. K. Rahner's thesis on the identity of the immanent
Trinity and of the economic Trinity: *Mysterium Salutis,*
Köln, 1961, t. II, pp. 327-329 and 370 *seq.*

90. Pius XII, AAS, 48 (1956), 327.

91. *Ibid.,* 310 (par. 3).

92. Saint Thomas Aquinas, *Summa Theologica,* I. 34. 2.

93. *Ibid.,* I. 32. 1. 1.

94. *Ibid.,* I. 41. 2.

95. *Ibid.* I. 41. 2. 2 (commentary on Col. 1, 13: the "beloved Son"). This doctrine of Saint Thomas is not a dogma of the Catholic Faith.

96. In this connection, Saint Thomas Aquinas has coined the splendid expression: "Verbum bonitatis" (*ibid.*, I. 27. 5. 2).

97. *Ibid.*, I. 43. 2. 2: "missio includit processionem aeternam, et aliquid addit, sc. temporalem effectum."

98. Saint Maximus the Confessor, PG, 90, 612 AB.

99. Mersch S.J., *op. cit.*, t. I, p. 285.

100. Cf. the second text referred to in note 87 of this chapter.

101. LG, 42 1; cf. Chapter Ten, C.

102. M. J. Lagrange O.P. (*Evangile selon saint Jean*, Paris, 1948⁸, pp. 185-187) translates the Greek "dia" here as *pour* and not *par*.

103. Cf. 1 Jn. 1, 3; Jn. 6, 44.

104. Saint Augustine, *de dono perseverantiae*, 14. 35; ML, 45, 1014.

105. *Ibid.*, 24. 67 (ML, 45, 1034): "Et illum et nos praedestinavit; quia et in illo ut esset caput nostrum et in nobis ut ejus corpus essemus, non praecessura merita nostra, sed opera sua futura praescivit." It is regrettable that Hans Urs von Balthasar, in his beautiful book, *Elizabeth de la Trinité* (Paris, 1960, pp. 37-87, notably 67-69), has seen fit to contrast social predestination and individual predestination, and to reject the latter. The doctrine of an irreducibly personal predestination cannot be set aside.

106. Saint Thomas Aquinas, *Summa Theologica*, III. 24. 4.

107. In his *De Praedestinatione Sanctorum*, 15, 30 (ML, 44, 981): "Est praeclarissimum lumen praedestinationis et gratiae ipse Salvator, Mediator Dei et hominum, Christus Jesus." On which Saint Thomas Aquinas splendidly comments: "Dicitur lumen praedestinationis et gratiae inquantum per ejus praedestinationem et gratiam manifestatur nostra praedestinatio" (*Summa Theologica*, III. 24. 3, *sed contra*): our predestination as members is manifested in that of our Head.

108. Jn. 6, 54.

109. Cf. DS, 1532, 1540, 1541, 1566 (DB, 801, 805, 806, 826).

110. Pius XII, *Haurietis Aquas*, par. 74 (AAS, 48, 1956, 346-347). The Pope adds: "In the devotion to the Sacred Heart, exterior works of piety are not given the first place, and its essential element does not consist in the benefits to be obtained; for if Christ the Lord saw fit to guarantee such benefits by private promises, this was done in order to urge men to fulfill with greater fervor the great duties of the Catholic religion—namely, love and expiation, and thereby to provide in the best possible way for their own spiritual growth." One notices the subtle quality of the idea: nothing is more effective than the pure love which relegates to the

second place, while not eliminating, temporal or spiritual personal interest. The idea and practice of reparation fosters this pure love.

111. See the text cited in the preceding note. On reparation, the following are useful: H. Rondet S.J.: "Le péché et la réparation dans le culte du Sacré-Coeur," in *Cor Jesu*, Rome, 1959, t. I, pp. 683-720; P. Hartmann S.C.J.: *Le sens plénier de la réparation du péché*, Apostolat de le Réparation, Louvain, 1955, pp. 250-293.

112. Dom Victor Warnach O.S.B., *Agape, die Liebe als Grundmotiv der Neutestamentlichen Theologie*, Düsseldorf, 1951. We are acquainted with Dom Warnach's ideas thanks to an article by B. Dumoulin, "Epistémologie et Théologie trinitaire," *Rex. des Sc. Relig.*, 41 (1967), 331-340.

113. Saint Thomas Aquinas reminds us, however, that this motivation must not be understood in an anthropomorphic manner (*Summa Theologica*, 19. 4): "(Deus) vult ergo hoc esse propter hoc; sed non propter hoc vult hoc." One could question whether the authors mentioned in the preceding note have sufficiently avoided this pitfall.

114. In reality, the human love of the Man-Jesus for His Father is still a gift of the Father to His only Son, just as is His divine love.

115. Saint Thomas Aquinas, *Super Evangelium S. Joannis Lectura, in Jo.* 10, 17 (Marietti, Rome, 1952, par. 1422): "Ipsam Dei delectionem nullus mereri potest sed effectum divinae delectionis mereri possumus per bona opera nostra. . . . Evidens signum delectionis est quod homo ex caritate faciat Dei mandata." What is involved here is a proof of the love of God for this man.

116. Saint Augustine makes this splendid commentary on Jn. 16, 27 ("The Father himself loves you because you have loved me"): "Hinc ergo factum est ut diligeremus quia delecti sumus. Prorsus donum Dei est diligere Deum. Ipse ut diligeretur dedit qui non dilectus dilexit. . . . Amat nos Pater quia nos amamus Filium: cum a Patre et a Filio acceperimus ut et Patrem amemus et Filium: diffundit enim caritatem in cordibus nostris amborum Spiritus (Rm. 5, 5), per quem Spiritum et Patrem amamus et Filium et quem Spiritum cum Patre amamus et Filio. Amorem itaque nostrum pium quo colimus Deum fecit Deus et vidit quia bonum est, ideo quippe amavit ipse quod fecit. Sed in nobis non faceret quod amaret nisi antequam id faceret nos amaret" (In Joannem, *tract*. 102. 5; PL, 35, 1898).

117. Saint Thomas Aquinas commentates on Jn. 16, 27 in the light of 1 Jn. 4, 10 (read as against the Vulgate which adds an adverb, "*prior* dilexit," absent from the original Greek text): "Probatio non est per causam sed est per signum, quia hoc ipsum quod nos Deum diligimus est signum quod ipse

amat nos. . . . Amare Christum inquantum a Deo exivit satis est evidens signum amoris Dei. Qui ergo amat Christum quia a Deo exivit amor ejus praecipue retorquetur in Deum Patrem: non autem si amat Christum inquantum hominem." This is an admirable observation, singularly relevant in our own day!
118. Cf. note 110 of this chapter.
119. Saint Thomas Aquinas, *Super Ev. S. Jo. lect., in Jo. 14, 21* (Marietti, Rome, 1952, par. 1936): a distinction drawn between "dilectio secundum quid" ("vult aliquod bonum particulare") and "dilectio simpliciter" ("omne bonum, ut habeat ipsum Deum"). The Saint adds: "Deus autem omnia causata diligit secundum quid quia omni creaturae vult aliquid bonum, etiam ipsis daemonibus, ut sc. vivant, et intelligant, et sint." Clearly, the absolute love of the giving of self without conditions is predestinating love.
120. Saint Thomas Aquinas, *Summa Theologica*, I. 21. 4. 1; *de Potentia*, 5. 4. 6.
121. Cf. C. Boyer S.J., *De gratia* (Rome, 1930, p. 273, par. 365): the doctrine of predestination "ante praevisa merita," upheld by Saint Robert Bellarmine following Saint Augustine, does not run counter to "congruism." What we say here is inspired more directly by Saint Thomas Aquinas's commentary on 1 Tm. 2, 4 ("God our Savior desires all men to be saved") where the Angelic Doctor presents the commentary of Saint John Damascene: God wills with an antecedent willing the salvation of all, and with a consequent willing the salvation of the predestined: *super Epist. Pauli Lectura, t. II, in 1 Tm.,* par. 62.
122. Pius XII, *Haurietis Aquas,* par. 64 (AAS, 48, 1956, 341-342: "cujus *omnia complectentis* plenitudinis Dei clarissima imago est ipsum Cor Christi Jesu: plenitudinem dicimus misericordiae, quae propria est Novi Testamente." The word "complecti" can have two meanings: "to embrace" and "to contain." The first meaning, no doubt implied here *in recto,* in no way excludes the second, at least *in obliquo.*
123. Cf. Chapter Four, note 135, of *Christ for the World.*
124. Pius XII, *Haurietis Aquas,* par. 21 (AAS, 48, 1956, 321).
125. *Ibid.,* par. 47 (Latin text, p. 334).
126. We are using a Teilhardian term, fully applicable to the Humanity of Christ if one considers its activity in relation to the Church.
127. LG, 7. 8.
128. Saint Bonaventure, "Sermo de Corpore Christi," *Opera,* t. 5 (Quarrachi, 1891, pp. 553-566); discussed by E. Longpré O.F.M. in "Eucharistie et union mystique selon la spiritualité franciscaine" (*Rev. d'Ascétique et de Mystique,* 25 (1949), 310-318.
129. See Longpré, *art. cit.,* pp. 322-327; and also the same author's article, "Eucharistie et expérience mystique," in

DSAM, t. IV, col. 1598-1601 (Paris, 1961).

130. A certain, perhaps unilateral, interpretation of Teilhard would tend to deny this.

131. Saint John of the Cross, *The Living Flame of Love,* third strophe, *sub fine.* In *The Spiritual Canticle* (strophe 27, no 2) this saint defines the spiritual marriage in a way which corresponds perfectly with the effect proper to the Eucharist when the communicant places no obstacle in the way of grace: "It is a complete transformation within the Beloved, a transformation in which the parties give themselves one to the other completely in a union of love as perfect as is possible in this life." Complete transformation, reciprocal union, mutual possession: these too are the effects of the sacramental grace of the Eucharist.

132. "Eucharistic Heart" is a symbolic expression, like that of "Heart of Jesus." Both expressions signify the loving person of Christ. If the former adds a shade of meaning to the latter, both use one of the words of the basic vocabulary of men, the word "heart," a word which designates a whole human composite, the innermost center of the person. The eschatological character of the symbol of the Eucharistic Heart results from the structure itself of the sacrament of the Eucharist, a sacrament which announces the glory to come and is its "prognostic" sign (Saint Thomas Aquinas, *Summa Theologica,* III. 64. 3).

133. Saint Francis de Sales: conclusion to "Treatise on the love of God."

134. Blessed Ruysbroeck, *L'anneau ou la pierre brillante,* chap. 12, published as an appendix to *L'ornement de noces spirituelles, Brussels,* 1920, p. 269.

135. After the Parousia, the Heart of Christ as such "will not cease to beat with its steady and peaceful rhythm (imperturbabile ac placido pulsu moveri) and still to signify the threefold love through which the Son of God is united to His heavenly Father and with the whole community of men"—because men will again be composites of bodies and souls, except that the bodies will be perfectly translucent signs of the souls. The quotation in the above sentence is from *Haurietis Aquas,* par. 34 (Latin text, pp. 328-329). Already in this first relationship, the Heart of Christ will continue to symbolize His threefold love. As wounded visibly and forever wounded, It will symbolize this love in an even stricter sense: through the visible wound, we shall see the incomprehensible character of the formerly invisible but henceforth visible wound of love (cf. *ibid.,* par. 52; Latin text, p. 337). Furthermore, Saint Thomas Aquinas (*Summa Theologica,* III. 54. 4. 3) clearly explains that Christ's body could change only by a new death: "unde patet quod cicatrices quas Christus post resurrectionem in suo corpore ostendit, numquam postmodum ab illius corpore

sunt remotae." The wound in Christ's side will be the sign of a suffering once undergone and never to return.

136. Cf. GS, 38. 1.

137. One could say that the Eucharistic Heart will remain forever the natural, even glorified, symbol of the trinitarian love. On the symbol, see K. Rahner S.J., *Schriften zur Theologie,* Koeln, 1960, t. IV, pp. 275-312.

138. We here define the object of the devotion paid by the Church to the Eucharistic Heart as the *twofold* act of Christ in instituting the Eucharist. A consequence both of the traditional doctrine concerning the divine-human works of Christ, and of the Church's condemnation of monoergism, is involved here (Cf. A. Michel, DTC, XV, 1, 1950, 205-216: art. *"théandrique, operation,"* and also DS, 268).

2

THE EUCHARISTIC HEART OF JESUS
GIVER OF THE OTHER PARACLETE,
THE SPIRIT OF TRUTH

A theme which has long exercised the minds of theologians is that concerning the relations between the (incarnate) Word and the Holy Spirit. To investigate this theme is certainly the most splendid of undertakings, but also the most difficult if one is to avoid certain brilliant but false formulations.

This theme can be dealt with in a basically trinitarian manner, or primarily from the viewpoint of Christology. It is the latter that we choose here.

Is it the Holy Spirit who sends Christ, or is it Christ who gives the Spirit? Is it Christ the Word or Christ the Word Incarnate who gives Him? What relation exists between the mystery of the Eucharist and the gift of the Spirit of Truth and of Love? Is the Holy Spirit symbolized by the Heart of Jesus? Has the Spirit played a role in the development of the cult of this Heart and, more especially, of this Eucharistic Heart?

Let us atempt to answer these questions in order, and to establish the connection between the answers; for it is through careful attention to the inter-relationships between mysteries that theology progresses.[1]

A. The Eucharistic Heart of Jesus,
Giver of the "Other Paraclete" (Jn. 14, 16)

It cannot be denied that the Holy Spirit has formed the Man-Jesus; for does not the Apostles' Creed proclaim that Christ was born of the Holy Spirit and of the Virgin Mary?

The Scriptures also show us that Christ was "driven" and sent by the Holy Spirit: "And Jesus, full of the Holy Spirit, returned from the Jordan, and was led by the Spirit for forty days in the wilderness" (Lk. 4, 1): ". . . he saw the heavens opened and the Spirit descending upon him like a dove. . . . The Spirit immediately drove him out into the wilderness" (Mk. 1, 10-12): "And Jesus returned in the power of the Spirit into Galilee, and . . . he came to Nazareth . . . and he went to the synagogue . . . and there was given to him the book of the prophet Isaiah. He opened the book and found the place where it was written, 'The Spirit of the Lord is upon me, because he has anointed me to preach good news to the poor. He has sent me to proclaim release to the captive and recovering of sight to the blind . . .'" (Lk. 4, 14-18).

Thus Christ presents Himself to us as the Emissary of the Spirit, as His Anointed, consecrated by the Unction, which is the Spirit Himself[2] and, although born of the Holy Spirit (cf. Lk. 1, 35), as having been filled by this Spirit in a new way[3] at His baptism, with a view to His mission.

However, the same Gospel of Saint Luke shows us the risen Christ promising to send the Spirit promised by the Father (Lk. 24, 49). The Gospel of Saint John, while in line with the synoptic Gospels as regards the descent of the Holy Spirit on Christ at His baptism, emphasizes the Christ who promises, breathes, sends the Spirit in whom He baptizes (Jn. 1, 32-34; 15, 26; 16, 7; 20, 22).

It is clear, therefore, that the Christ of Saint John's Gospel is much more He who sends the Spirit, than He who is sent by this Spirit.

Saint Thomas Aquinas is in perfect harmony with the Gospel and with his own doctrine of the mission of the Divine Persons, a doctrine itself also rooted in this datum, when he refuses to see, in Saint Luke's expressions concerning the sending of Christ by the Spirit, the indication of a sending, properly so called, of the Son by the Third Divine Person.[4]

Clearly, it is impossible that the Spirit, proceeding from the only Son to whom He owes His eternal origin, could be the origin of that Son. On the other hand, however, there is nothing to prevent our saying that the Holy Spirit, like the Father and the Son, is the principle of the redemptive work accomplished by Christ.

On the contrary, the Son sends the Spirit in the strictest sense of the verb. The Word, Co-breather with the Father of their only Spirit, sends this Spirit to men, in an extension of His uncreated act of breathing Him. The same Word of the divine Goodness, in perfect union with His Father, loves Their common lovableness, and thus eternally produces their Spirit of Love—the Spirit whom They both send, in the absolute simplicity of the same eternity, to mortal men. The Holy Spirit is eternally sent in time.

Some theologians[5] have recently affirmed that Christ *as man* gives and sends the Spirit to men. They have interpreted in this sense the statement in Saint John's Gospel: ". . . he breathed on them, and said to them. 'Receive the Holy Spirit' " (20, 22). These theologians, it seems to us, do not express themselves very happily.

In effect, the eternal procession is connoted by the temporal mission.[6] If the Man-Jesus, precisely as man, gave and sent the Spirit, this would necessarily imply that the Creator would proceed from the creature, and thereby God's transcendence would be destroyed. But we are not to be taken as saying that all is false in these theologians' statement.

Saint Thomas Aquinas has splendidly developed

the element of truth which it contains. Focusing on an idea of Saint Augustine, he writes:

> To give grace or the Holy Spirit belongs to Christ as He is God, authoritatively; but instrumentally it belongs also to Him as man, inasmuch as His manhood is the instrument of His Godhead. And hence by the power of the Godhead His actions were beneficial—i.e., by causing grace in us, both meritoriously and efficiently. But Augustine denies that Christ as man gives the Holy Spirit authoritatively. Even other saints are said to give the Holy Spirit instrumentally, or ministerially . . .[7]

One notes his distinction: the Man-Jesus gives the Spirit, but it is not *as man*[8] that He does so; He gives the Spirit "inasmuch as His manhood is the instrument of His Godhead" in the work of Redemption. The Man-Jesus, who in the unity of His Person is the Word of God, breathes and sends the Spirit whom His "manhood" does not breathe or send. The humanity of Jesus gives the Spirit, not on the mere authority of His human nature, but on the authority of that nature as assumed by a divine Person.[9]

Or, if one prefers, the humanity of Christ is only the instrumental cause, and not the secondary cause, of the giving of the Spirit. In this connection, we remind ourselves that the instrumental action as such does not belong to the instrument, whereas the action of the secondary cause is truly its own, though of course in absolute dependence on the primary Cause.[10]

Clearly, the humanity of the Risen Christ is the instrument of the gift of the Spirit in a different although similar way, by comparison with the instrumentality of the saints to which the Angelic Doctor refers in the text quoted above. The human free will of Christ is a primary instrumental cause, while His psychological or physical powers actuated by this free will, are secondary instrumental causes; whereas the ministers of the sacraments are distinct instrumental causes.

If Jesus, as man, receives the Spirit and, as man assumed by the Word, i.e. through His humanity as instrument of the Word, gives this Spirit, it is purely and simply as the Word that He gives Him, as being the eternal origin of the Spirit and as He who sends the Spirit in time. But, as Father Le Guillou rightly emphasizes,[11] it is the incarnate Word, in the unity of His being, who sends this Spirit.

Another Dominican theologian, Father Guérard des Lauriers, also focuses this point and a part of the matter in question:

> Although it is as God that Christ sends the Spirit, nevertheless the human nature subsists in the Word producing the Spirit—in this very act which belongs to the Person of the Word and which produces the Spirit. . . . Using the language of psychology, we could also say that the sacred humanity is completely present to the Word that breathes the Spirit, and that this sacred humanity thus assists in the breathing which it does not produce in a human way, but in which it subsists inasmuch as this humanity has been assumed by the Divinity.
>
> The intuition of Saint Cyril, expressed in the formula which now reads strangely, "mia phusis tou logou sesarkôménè," tends to link up with this mystery. Because of refinements established since his day, we no longer say that Christ has a unitary nature,[13] but that He is a reality one and incarnate, that is, admitting of human nature. Consequently, in accordance with the unity and with the wholeness of Christ's Being, this reality always underlies every operation which emanates from it. Although they are distinct, Christ's two natures do not divide His *esse:* this *esse* belongs formally to the Word, but it remains true that the sacred humanity does not have an *esse* which could be part of this simple *esse*. It follows that, in fact, the sacred humanity is inseparable from whatever subsists in accordance with this simple *esse*, and in particular inseparable from the divine opera-

tion by which the Holy Spirit proceeds and is sent.[14]

It must be maintained, therefore, that inasmuch as Christ is a reality one and incarnate, His human nature, especially after the Resurrection,[15] cannot be excluded from the sending of the Holy Spirit.

We can now take the matter further, with Dom H. M. Diepen and in the light of the encyclical *Haurietis Aquas:*

> The sacred Humanity is the instrumental cause of the pouring forth of the Holy Spirit. . . . The Paraclete proceeds eternally from the uncreated Love of the Son. The hypostatic union of the human will of Christ with this divine Love, and the harmonious unity of the Person of the Incarnate Word, make His human heart the special instrument for the pouring forth of the Paraclete. It is by His human intelligence that Christ communicates to us the mysteries which He contemplates in the bosom of the Father; equally, it is through His Sacred Heart that He gives the Spirit who proceeds from His eternal Love.[16]

This being so, one understands how Pius XII could write: "love is the gift of the Heart of Christ and of His Spirit"[17]; "est enim haec caritas Jesu Cordis ejusque Spiritus donum." Thus Pius XII regards the Holy Spirit as the Spirit of the Heart of Jesus. He connects this with the explicit doctrine of Christ Himself, showing us how the Church drinks the Spirit and the rivers of living waters which flow from the Heart of Christ, to whom the Church, thanks to the "inestimable gift" of the devotion to this Heart, can manifest a more ardent love:

> Enriched with this inestimable gift, the Church can manifest to its divine founder a more ardent love, and thus realize more fully this wish which Saint John ascribes to Christ Himself: "On the last day of the feast, the great day, Jesus stood

up and proclaimed, 'If anyone thirst, let him
come to me and drink. He who believes in me,
as Scripture has said, *Out of his heart shall flow
rivers of living water.*' Now this he said about
the Spirit, which those who believed in him were
to receive" (Jn. 7, 37-39). Those who were lis-
tening to Him would surely have associated this
promise of a spring of "living water" flowing
from His side, with the prophetic words of Isaiah,
Ezechiel, and Zechariah concerning the Mes-
sianic kingdom, and also with the symbolic stone
which miraculously emitted a jet of water when
Moses struck it.[20]

Thus, as Pius XII quite clearly informs us, the Holy
Spirit "flows from the side of Christ." A little further
on, he develops magnificently the Gospel image: "He
alone, the Word made flesh, full of grace and truth,
come among men crushed with the weight of their sins
and their miseries, can cause to spring from His human nature, hypostatically united with His divine Person, a spring of living water to irrigate the parched
earth of humanity, so as to make of it a flourishing
and fertile garden."[21] The garden is, clearly, the
Church as irrigated by the River of life "flowing from
the throne of God and of the Lamb" (Rev. 22, 1).

These texts provide the New Testament basis for
Pius XII's statement that the Paraclete is the Spirit
of Jesus, the Breath of the Heart of Jesus. This com-
plements by contrast another statement in the same
encyclical: the Spirit that flows from the side of the
crucified Christ is also He whose operation has formed
the Heart of Jesus in the womb of the Virgin Mary.[22]

Dom Diepen has well synthesized these different
aspects:

The Holy Spirit is, by personal attribute, the
immanent product of the uncreated love of
Christ. He is, by appropriation, the efficient
principle of His created love and of His Heart.
He is, by personal attribute, the supreme gift of
Christ—the gift merited by His human love,

spread by His divine love and by His human love
and even by His human heart: the Gift, therefore, of the triple love of Christ; in short, the
Gift of the Sacred Heart.[23]

It is therefore the human and sensible love of the
Redeemer which gives and spreads, under the sacramental symbols of water and of blood, and as the
instrument of the divine and supra-sensible Word, the
Holy Spirit that is the immanent.product of His uncreated love. The human love of a divine Person gives
the divine fruit of His divine Love.

The pierced Heart of Jesus is therefore the symbol
and the sign of the Spirit of Love whom It gives and
contains.[24] This Heart is, for sinful mankind who re-
sists It, the most evocative sign of the love of the Spirit
of Truth.

To be precise, the Heart of Jesus instrumentally
gives the Holy Spirit as Spirit of Truth and loving
Revealer of hidden mysteries, through the sacramental
charisms of confirmation and of the episcopate.[25]

But these sacraments are polarized by the Eucharist,
their *raison d'être*. Confirmation involves, above all, a
declaration of faith in the mystery which brings together all the other mysteries: the Eucharist.[26] The
episcopate as sacrament signifies and instrumentally
realizes the unity around the Eucharistic table.[27] On
the other hand, the Heart of Jesus—which, as instrument of the Word, spreads the Spirit—acts now in
the Church preeminently through the mystery of the
Eucharist. Through the Eucharist, the Heart of the
Lamb comes "to re-activate" the sacramental graces
of confirmation and of the episcopate. In the Eucharist,
Christ immolates Himself anew and offers Himself to
the Father in order to fill us with Their Spirit, in
Communion. It is preeminently through the Eucharist
that we receive and drink the Spirit (cf. 1 Cor., 12,
13).[28] To use a favorite image of the Greek Fathers,
and notably of Saint John Damascene,[29] the Eucharist
is the burning coal of the Divinity in which glows the

Fire of the Spirit which Christ came to kindle (cf. Is.
6, 6-7; Lk. 12, 49). Scheeben has dealt splendidly and
at considerable length with this theme of the Christ
who, through the Eucharist, regales us and fills us
with His Spirit.[30]

We can say without hesitation, therefore, that the
Eucharistic Heart of Jesus gives to the pilgrim Church
the Spirit of Truth, the other Paraclete. It immolates
Itself in order to give this Spirit to the Church (cf.
Jn. 14, 16) in the sacramental sign of Its Blood.
This is at once a gift by last will and testament and
a gift of the living, if one may use (as indeed the
New Testament does) legal terms in relation to this
mystery. And the Eucharistic Heart gives the Paraclete in the Eucharist. Precisely as sacramental, our
Communions are therefore spiritual in the sense that
they enable us to commune with the Holy Spirit
through the spiritualized flesh of Christ. Each of our
sacramental and spiritual (in every sense of this latter adjective[31]) Communions quicken in us the gifts
of faith-grounded love which are received at our confirmation. Although in itself the flesh can achieve nothing, the Spirit vivifies through the flesh of Christ, the
Word made flesh, delivered for the life of the world—
a life which cannot be obtained if one does not eat
this spiritualized flesh (Jn. 6, 63; 1, 14; 6, 51. 54. 57;
1 Cor. 15, 44).[32]

It might be objected that, while all this is true,
the love that is grounded on faith is a gift which is
appropriated to the Holy Spirit, and which is also given
by the Father and the Son. Yes, indeed. But Saint
Thomas defines "appropriation" as "a manifestation
of the divine Persons by the use of essential attributes":
its function therefore is to manifest the personal property of a divine Person.[33]   In specially attributing
to the Holy Spirit the gift of the love that is grounded
on faith, we give real expression to the idea that the
Third Person is the Breath of the reciprocal Love of
the Father and of the Son—the personal Love in God,
the fruit of the Love which the Father and the Son

have, as a single principle, for their own Truth; and
that therefore the Third Person is the Spirit of Truth.
Consequently, in saying that the Eucharist Heart of
the Lamb gives the Spirit of Truth, we are proclaim-
ing the lovable splendor of the truth of the trinitarian
mystery.

One thus understands more clearly how Vatican II
could say: "Christ is now at work in the hearts of
men through the energy of His Spirit."[34] But, re-
ciprocally, it is equally true to say—and this is something we have now to consider—that the Spirit of
Jesus draws men to the Eucharistic Heart, symbol
of the Paraclete's love for errant mankind.

B. The Spirit of Truth Draws Mankind to the Heart and the Eucharistic Heart of Jesus

Among the many ways in which the Holy Spirit
assists the Church of which He is the soul, we must
certainly include the schools of spirituality and the
growth of Catholic worship.

The whole history of the birth and gradual growth
of the cult of the Sacred Heart of Jesus unveils to
eyes of faith the action of the Spirit who glorifies
Christ (cf. Jn. 16, 14).

Bearing in mind what "appropriation" means, as
we have seen above, one readily accepts that this
progress can be appropriated in a special way to the
Spirit of Love. If, with Pius XII, one acknowledges
the cult of the Sacred Heart as an inestimable gift
which enables the Church to love its Spouse more perfectly, how can one fail to attribute the origin of this
cult to Him who is the personal Love between the
Father and the Son?

The Spirit is the author of the Scriptures which already invite us, at least implicitly, to cultivate this
devotion to the Heart of Jesus.[35] The same Spirit
has aroused the medieval mystics (Bonaventure, Catherine of Siena, Suso), and then those of the Counter-
Reformation (John Eudes, Margaret Mary), through

whom this cult has gradually developed, first among the spiritual élite, then among the Catholic masses; but the latter development really took place only when the Holy See took up a decisive attitude towards it.

In connection with this long history, one can also accept as true the general observation made by Father Holstein as regards the "pneumatic" origin of the development of the dogma:

> The special grace bestowed by the Holy Spirit on the Catholic hierarchy, is that of discerning and judging the Christian sense of the faithful, of recognizing tradition in that sense, and of explicitly proclaiming the lived faith when the Spirit judges that the time is ripe.
>
> The same Spirit who inspired Scripture in order to give us the Revelation, inspires[36] the Church in its complex and infrangible unity, to understand this Scripture in order that it may grasp fully the Revelation contained therein, and accept it in faith. He inspires the devotion of the faithful by giving them the sense of faith; and He enlightens the theologians that they may formulate, justify, clarify this faith which they themselves protect and of which they are living examples. And He gives to the magisterium to proclaim the living Tradition of which He is the faithful interpreter.[37]

Today, we can more clearly see that the Spirit of the Father was urging, first the faithful, then the magisterium, towards the Heart of the Son. After having induced the private cult, He aroused the explicit public cult of the pierced Heart of the Redeemer. This stage reached its culmination in 1856, when Pius IX extended to the universal Church (of the Latin rite) the feast of the Sacred Heart. Then, thanks to a great collective effort of Catholic theologians who had prepared the way, the magisterium, in 1928 and in 1956, was able to specify in memorable encyclicals the doctrinal import of this cult. In this very homogeneous evolution, the Spirit has been constantly active.

An analogous pattern of development could be traced in connection with the private cult of the Eucharistic Heart of Jesus, in the Church. Initially, early in the second half of the nineteenth century, the time when it blossomed, it met with some resistance. Nevertheless, by 1890, one could already count 14 pontifical documents favorable to the devotion to the Eucharistic Heart.[38] After new restrictive measures taken by the Holy See, measures now lapsed except for one of them,[39] the Church introduced the feast of the Eucharistic Heart of Jesus, not automatically to the whole Church, however.[40] Then, in the encyclical *Haurietis Aquas*, the Church solemnly recognized the duty of the cult to the Eucharistic Heart. Let us recall lines we have already quoted, in order to consider them in a new context:

> One cannot readily accept the strength of the love which urged Christ to give Himself to us as spiritual food, except through honoring with a particular cult the Eucharistic Heart of Jesus.[41]

Clearly, we have a real duty to grasp, as perfectly as possible, the strength of this oblative and sacrificial love which is at the origin of our Eucharistic eating of Christ. Consequently, the private cult of the Eucharistic Heart, and a particular cult which gives more specific focus to the more general cult of the Heart of Jesus, is also a real and delightful obligation recognized and accepted by us in grateful love. However, this does not rule out a previous statement in another document of the Holy See: "The cult of the Sacred Heart in the Eucharist is not more perfect than that of the Eucharist, nor is it different from the cult of the Sacred Heart."[42] But the text of Pius XII, carrying as it does the more solemn authority of an encyclical, stresses more clearly perhaps that a cult involves "an essential attitude of religion and of love, characterizing our relations with God in Christ."[43]

The cult of the Eucharistic Heart of Jesus serves to complete and to specify the cult of the Sacred Heart, by particularizing it.

Such a cult would not be approved or made public in the Church or presented as obligatory by the Church, unless through the action of the Spirit of Love, of that eternal Spirit in whom and under whose pressure the incarnate Son offers Himself to the Father. The help the Spirit gives to the Church, His body that He ceaselessly animates, shows itself in the progressive and increasing approbation of this devotion leading up to this "particular cult."

What is the design thus pursued by the Spirit, who comes from the Father and the Son and who glorifies Them both? Although no one knows "whither . . . goes" anyone "who is born of the Spirit" (cf. Jn. 3, 8) or the Church born of Him, we nevertheless hear the voice of the Spirit through and with the Church. It seems to us that first the progress and then the solemn approval of the cult of the Eucharistic Heart constitute for the theologian a "sign of the times." These things signify what the Spirit wills for the Church of our age—namely, that there should be concentrated theological reflection and heightened spiritual life centered on the mystery of the Eucharist, synthesis of Revelation, in the ardent light of love. While the devotion to the Eucharistic Heart is not more sublime than the devotion simply to the Sacred Heart, nevertheless the first more effectively promotes theological synthesis.

It even seems to us that the complex symbolism of the Eucharistic Heart, to which we shall return shortly, links up in the scope of its synthesis with the basic intuitions of Cyril of Alexandria. The two words, "Eucharistic Heart," sensitively express, of course in a different context, what the great Doctor of the Incarnation had in mind: a unified vision of the Trinity, of the Redemptive Incarnation and of the Church, bringing these mysteries together in that of the Eucharist. It is this unified vision which our era is yearning to recover, and it could well be the will of the Holy Spirit that we should re-discover it under the symbolism of the Eucharistic Heart, in the light of Saint Cyril. It is useful therefore to recall and to consider some of his texts.

The primordial idea of Saint Cyril is that the Spirit leads us to the Son, who is present in the Eucharist and through whom we have, together, access to the Father. "Our return to God, which is achieved through Christ our Savior, occurs only in the communion and the sanctification of the Spirit. It is the Spirit who raises us to the Son and thus unites us with God. In receiving Him into our souls, we become participants and communicants in the divine nature. We receive Him through the Son, and, in the Son, we receive the Father."[44]

The Spirit leads us to the only Son, but it is the Son who gives us the Spirit. Is not that exactly what we have brought out when dealing with the relationship between the Spirit, the Eucharist, and ourselves?

In Saint Cyril's view, the Son "receives" the Spirit in order to give Him to us: "Although He possesses the Spirit, it is nevertheless said that the Spirit has been given to the Son in order that, in the Son, we should all receive the Spirit. It is with this aim that the Son assumes the descent from Abraham and that He becomes like in all things to His brethren. It is not for Himself that He, the only Son, receives the Holy Spirit, because the Spirit is to Him, in Him, and through Him."[45]

Saint Cyril holds that we are spiritually united with Christ through His Spirit, and physically united with Him through the eating of His flesh. In the same way, we are united one with another. Again, Saint Cyril writes:

> First Christ comes physically, as man, mingling and uniting Himself with us through the mystic communion; but spiritually also, as God, through the power and love of His Spirit, who

comes within us to infuse us with a new life and to make us sharers of His divine nature.[46]

It is interesting to notice the parallelism (of Platonic tinge) between the flesh and the Spirit shown by this text, a parallelism to which Cyril seems to hold, though this does not lead him to maintain the existence of an organic union between the two, or of an instrumental causality of the physical union with the Eucharistic Christ in relation to the pouring forth of the Spirit in us. Like Augustine, Cyril seems to ignore the idea of instrumental causality.[47] Underlying what he says,[48] and indeed serving as an horizon to his thought, is the idea that the physical breath, itself spiritualized, of the Risen Christ exhales the Spirit. Or, in our categories and in accordance with our symbolism (in which the nature of man and the Biblical language blend harmoniously), it is the Eucharistic and spiritualized Heart of Christ, the Anointed of the Spirit,[49] that gives us this Spirit in and through the Blood that still flows from It.

Whatever one might say about the anthropology of Saint Cyril and the way it conditions his theology, it remains true that he brought together, in the harmony of a splendid synthesis, the mysteries of the Trinity, of the Redemptive Incarnation, of the Eucharist, of grace, and of the Church, viewed together in the light of Saint John, on whose Gospel he is, with Augustine, the deepest of commentators. We believe that the Spirit of the Lamb, desiring to restore to the Church of the twentieth century a global vision recapitulated in all its aspects through a single symbol, has led the Church to declare the need for a particular cult of the Eucharistic Heart of Jesus.

This symbol, we have said, is complex. We shall see why the Eucharistic Heart is a very attractive and highly rich symbol of the mystery of the love of the Person of the Paraclete, in His eternal procession and in His temporal mission.

First, let us remind ourselves[50] that already the

Heart of Jesus signifies (though indirectly[51]) the eternal and reciprocal[52] Love between the Father and the Son, from which springs eternally the personal Love who is Their Spirit: an eternal intra-divine Love which is the condition and the origin of the love of the Holy Spirit for the sinful human race. "The cult of the Sacred Heart is none other than the cult of the love which the Holy Spirit lavishes upon sinful men", writes Pius XII.[53] The human heart of the incarnate Word is a much more expressive symbol of the love of the "other Paraclete" (Jn. 14, 16) than is that of the dove, of water, of wind, or of fire. On the one hand, human love better symbolizes the intra-divine and extra-divine personal Love than do these cosmic things; and on the other hand, human love includes in itself or connotes nearly all those things which it places at its service or through which it expresses itself. If the Heart of Jesus is an indirect image of the Breath of the Father and of the Son, one could say that the human breath of the Heart of the Risen Jesus, with the love that produces it, is the most direct image of that divine Breath. The breath through which Jesus has willed to represent to us the Person of His Spirit, is, within man, a yearning sigh by which his love, and therefore his heart, overflows, produced as it is by the intensity of his love. The Holy Spirit is a Breath of Love who issues from the Father and from the Son,[55] and whom the human heart of the Son gives and spreads when His Resurrection, by the power of this divine Spirit, has made Him "the last Adam become a life-giving spirit" (cf. 1 Cor. 15, 44-45). It can be said that Christ, by deliberately and freely[56] choosing in fidelity to the whole Biblical tradition the symbol of His human and loving[57] breath in order to designate the Third Person of the Trinity, was intending to link Him with the natural symbol of His own human heart as the direct expression of His love, and as the indirect expression of the love of this Spirit.

If already the symbol of the Heart of Jesus carries a rich pneumatological significance, even richer is that of the Eucharistic Heart. With the symbol of the heart, the expression associates the not less anthropological symbol of the spiritualized bread and wine of the Eucharistic mystery which is a sacrament—i.e. the visible sign of an invisible reality. In uniting among themselves the hearts of the communicants, so as to make them to be as "one heart" (Acts 4, 32), the Eucharistic Heart of Jesus symbolizes the Spirit, who is the consubstantial[58] and invisible communion between the Father and the Son. Con-corporal and consanguine one with the other, consummated in one because they eat the flesh of the Son of man and drink His Blood, they are thus an instrument through whom the world believes that the Father has sent His Son and that these Two are one in and through the Spirit (cf. Jn. 6 and 17, *passim*). The Eucharistic Heart symbolizes the Spirit of Love who loves the world to which He is sent by the Father and the Son, from whom He proceeds and whose bond of unity He is. It is a symbolism whose medium is the symbolic mystery of the unity of the Church, image of the unity of the triune God in the Spirit as well as being its effect.

But the Eucharistic Heart is not only the "visible"[59] sign of "the unity of the Spirit in the bond of peace" (Eph. 4, 3); this Heart is also the Mediator containing and giving this Spirit. This is what, in full continuity with the Eastern and Western patristic tradition,[60] the new canons of the Latin rite bring out: "In nourishing ourselves with the Body and Blood of Your Son, may we be filled with His Spirit, so as to become visibly one body and one soul in Christ."[61] The liturgy itself, therefore, bears witness to this truth that the Blood of Christ fills us with His Spirit. There is nothing surprising in this, since Jesus already implied as much: "He who eats my flesh and drinks my blood has eternal life. . . . If anyone thirst, let him come to me and drink. He who believes in me, as Scripture has said, 'Out of his heart shall flow rivers of living water'" (Jn. 6, 54; 7, 37-39). The Blood that flows from the Heart of the Lamb is presented by Him as a symbol of His Spirit—as a sacramental symbol that not only signifies but also contains this Spirit.[62] The Blood is therefore a direct symbol, the Heart an indirect symbol, of the Spirit.

The New Testament also indicates to us that the wine, like blood but in a very different manner, is the symbol of the Holy Spirit (Eph. 5, 18; Acts 2, 13). The wine, a product of man's work on something which is the free gift of God, supplies the matter which the words of Christ, in the power of the Spirit, transubstantiate into His precious Blood. Wine intoxicates: the Blood of Christ, in which we drink the Spirit, produces the ecstasy of love. The Eucharistic and bloody Heart of Christ, in signifying and giving the Spirit, connotes the cosmos from which It derives its conditions of existence and which aspires, through It, to its transfiguration. This Heart also connotes the Church which It fills with the Spirit and which It associates through this pouring forth of the Spirit, with Its redemptive sacrifice. Finally, It connotes Its own Parousia through which, by transfiguring the world, it will consummate the Church, fully unveiling to it the Spirit who is its soul and its life-giving drink.

We see more clearly, therefore, why the Spirit leads the Church to adore His own symbol in the Eucharistic Heart of the Redeemer. Does He not thus offer to the Church a particularly rich sign of His love, a daily renewed sign of the communion of the Father and the Son that is the Spirit Himself, of the Redemptive Incarnation, of the Church as a communion-in-love of all the coredeemers, and of the cosmos which He creates and transfigures, first by the love which He pours into human hearts, and then definitively on the Last Day through the humanity of His Anointed? For all these mysteries are symbolized and brought together in the Eucharistic Heart of the Redeemer.

When one considers the matter, is not the way in which the private cult of the Eucharistic Heart of the Lamb has grown up in the Church, a singular manifestation of the merciful love of the Spirit for the Church?

Does not this cult present the Spirit, already a Gift of the Heart of Jesus, as a new and inestimate Gift of this immolated Lamb to His Spouse?—a more particular Gift within the general gift of His Heart? In fostering this devotion, we enable the Church "to manifest to its divine founder a more ardent love,"[63] and to drink more copiously the Spirit that flows, with the Blood, from His ever open Heart.

It is in connection with the Eucharistic Heart that these words of Paul VI are verified more particularly:

> In the Sacred Heart of Jesus are to be found the origin and the principle of the sacred liturgy, since this Heart is the holy temple of God whence there rises up to the Father the sacrifice of expiation which can save those who through it come to God (cf. Heb. 7, 25). Furthermore, it is this Heart that incites the Church to seek every means by which our separated brethren may come into full unity with the Chair of Peter, and by which even those who are not yet Christians may also know with us the only true God, and Jesus Christ whom He has sent (Jn. 17, 3).

Was Cardinal Amette, Archbishop of Paris, wrong when he wrote in 1903: "The cult to the Eucharistic Heart is the purest and fullest blossoming of the devotion to the Sacred Heart"?[65] Was Benedict XV misled when he prophesied: "The devotion to the Eucharistic Heart will be a source of graces for souls; it will spread more and more in the Church"?[66] Did not Pius XII validate this prophecy when, in formally recognizing this cult with all the solemnity of an encyclical, he used these words which we again quote: "One cannot readily grasp the strength of the love which urged Christ to give Himself to us as spiritual food, except through honoring with a particular cult the Eucharistic Heart of Jesus"? More than even, will not the Church of the future concentrate its dogmatic, liturgical, and moral effort on that sun which, through the Spirit, ceaselessly enlightens and enfolds it—the sun that is the Eucharistic Heart of Jesus, the Lamb of God?

Appendix: Eucharist and Holy Spirit according to Scheeben

The Eucharist realizes above all the most real and most perfect external mission of the Divine Persons.

The Holy Spirit, Spirit of the Son, is united in a very real way with the body of the Son in whom He reposes and dwells. Similarly, He comes to us in this body, in order to unite Himself with us and to communicate Himself to us. In the body of the Logos that He fills, we receive the Holy Spirit at the very source, so to speak, whence it springs; like the blood, the Holy Spirit spreads Himself from the Heart into the other members, from the real body of the Logos into the members of His mystical Body who are substantially united with Him. . . .

The distinction and the relationship between the mission of the Son and that of the Holy Spirit are, as we have already indicated, already expressed in the Eucharistic species. The species of wine (symbol of the blood) with its liquidity, its warmth, its comforting and pleasant bouquet, its enlivening quality, represents the Holy Spirit, whose procession is a springing up from the Father and the Son, and whose mission is a pouring forth which is in itself the river and the sweet odor of the divine life. This species represents him as the wine that springs up from the Logos as from a divine cluster of grapes, the wine of ardent love, of strength and of life, of intoxicating beatitude, the wine that has been pressed out in the sacred blood of the human heart of the Logos by the great strength of His love, that has been spread over the world and poured into us in this blood.

Although the Holy Spirit is sent by the Son and comes to us in the Son, He is nevertheless, by the strongest of appropriations, the channel through whom the Son is introduced into us.

As the Breath of His love, He urges the Son to give Himself to us in the Incarnation and in the Eucharist; as the fire of His sanctifying and unifying ardor, He effects within the womb of the Virgin the origin, the hypostatic union, and the holiness of the human nature of the Son; and, in the Eucharist, the transformation of earthly substances into those of His Flesh and His Blood. After the hypostatic union and the transubstantiation, He dwells with His warmth and His vital force in the flesh and blood of the Son of God from whom He proceeds, and He fills them with His essence in order to sanctify and to glorify them. In the Eucharist, above all, He glorifies and spiritualizes them, as a burning coal, so that they themselves appear as fire, as pure spirit. He makes use of this flesh and blood as of an instrument to manifest His sanctifying and glorifying power to all those who enter into contact with them; as of an organ to communicate Himself to all those who receive this flesh and this blood.

The body of Christ has *sprung* from the fire of the Holy Spirit, as a spiritual gift which God gives to us and which we in our turn offer in sacrifice. It is *penetrated* and *enfolded* by the Holy Spirit who glorifies and spiritualizes it, in such a way that the fire and the kindled coals appear to be one and the same. Finally, the body of Christ overflows with the Holy Spirit, spreading His sweet odor in the Mass, and His life-living power in Communion.

Those relations of the Eucharist with the Holy Spirit are best expressed by the image of the glowing coal, an image by which the Eastern Fathers and the liturgies love to designate the Eucharist. The very name *Eucharist* already indicates these relations, for does it not mean *the preeminent gift*, which flows from the Holy Spirit, Himself the gift *par excellence*, the gift that contains the Holy Spirit, with His essence and His power? How beautiful and meaningful was not the ancient custom of reserving the Eucharist in the *peristerium,* a dove-shaped vase, symbolizing the Holy Spirit! How well this symbolizes the Holy Spirit who brings to us the gift contained in this vase, and who dwells in this gift with His essence and His power, enfolding and penetrating it as the fire enfolds and penetrates the coal.

M. J. Scheeben, *The Mysteries of Christianity,* St. Louis, 1958, par. 75, pp. 528-530. On the peristerium, see: H. Leclercq, "Colombe eucharistique" in *Diction. d'Archéologie chrétienne et de Liturgie,* t. III, Paris, 1913, col. 2231-2234.

NOTES TO CHAPTER TWO

1. Cf. DS, 3016 (DB, 1796). The principle enunciated is very specially valid for examining the links between redemptive Incarnation and Trinity.

2. See Chapter Ten, note 13, and the text to which it refers. Pius XII teaches that the Son of God adorned His soul with this Spirit of grace and of Truth already in the immaculate womb of the Virgin (AAS, 35, 1943, 219).

3. It must be accepted that the humanity of Christ was filled from the first moment of its existence with the Holy Spirit who dwelt in it. Saint Thomas Aquinas held that no increase of grace occurred in Christ. J. Maritain thinks, however, that the grace of the *Christus viator,* complete of its kind, "did not cease to grow throughout His earthly life" (*De la Grace et de l'Humanité de Jesus,* Bruges, 1967, p. 89). If that is true, then baptism would have been a specific moment of that growth. If not, it may be admitted that the sacred Humanity of Jesus received, at that moment, a transient actual grace more closely preparing Him for the mission of His public life. Therefore He appears "full of the Holy Spirit" (Lk. 4, 1).

4. Saint Thomas Aquinas, *Summa Theologica,* I. 43. 8; cf. I, 43. 2. 3.

5. See, e.g., E. Schillebeeckx O.P., "Ascension and Pentecost," *Worship* 35 (1961), 352 ff.; E. Mersch, *op. cit.,* t. II, pp. 124-241.

6. Cf. H. F. Dondaine O.P., in his edition of the treatise *La Trinité* in the *Summa Theologica* of Saint Thomas Aquinas, Paris, Cerf, 1946, t. II, pp. 425-431.

7. Saint Thomas Aquinas, *Summa Theologica,* III. 8. 1. 1. Saint Thomas gently contradicts Saint Augustine who, it seemed to him, always ignored the idea of instrumental causality. In his commentary on Gal. 3, 5, Saint Thomas specifies: "Spiritus Sanctus datur a solo Patre et Filio secundum quod ejus auctoritatem habent, non quidem dominii sed originis, quia ab utroque procedit" (*Super Ep. S. Pauli lectura,* I, Marietti, Rome, 1953, p. 594, par. 127). If, in this sense, the Holy Spirit does not Himself give Himself, it is not surprising that in the same connection, Christ as man cannot give the Holy Spirit. Saint Augustine deals with the subject in his *De Trinitate,* I. 12 and XV. 26. For him, the Risen Christ's act of breathing on the Apostles signifies that the Spirit proceeds eternally from the divine Person of the Son, but not that the Spirit is sent by the incarnate Word, or even given by Him as man. The idea of instrumental causality was to enable Saint Thomas to be the faithful interpreter of all the shades of meaning in the sacred text.

8. We mean: in as much as His humanity would be the *secondary* cause of such a gift.

9. Cf. the "rules of language" developed by Catholic theology concerning Christ, for example in the *Summa Theologica* of Saint Thomas Aquinas, III. 16. 5, 10.

10. On instrumental causality as distinct from secondary causality, see J. de Finance S.J., *Connaissance de l'Etre,* Paris-Bruges, 1966, par. 94, pp. 388-389. It must also be observed that, in the case considered here, the instrument used by the divine Person of the Word is a supernatural instrument causing an effect which infinitely exceeds it, just as it exceeds all the forces of nature. Cf. Saint Thomas Aquinas, III. 19. 1, 2; 48. 6.

11. M. J. Le Guillou O.P., encyclopedia *Catholicisme,* art. "Esprit-Saint," Paris, 1954, t. IV, col. 492.

12. A formula which Father Guérard de Lauriers, not without reason, prefers to translate as "a single and incarnate nature," and not as "a single nature incarnate." However, notice one important and rarely emphasized point: the local Lateran Council, in 649, of whose doctrinal authority we are aware because of the approbation of Pope Saint Martin I, retained and interpreted the famous formula of Saint Cyril concerning the "one nature," at the same time as it admitted the two-natures (diphysite) formula of Chalcedon (DS, 505-506; DB, 258-259): "incarnata dicitur nostra substantia perfecte in Christo Deo et indiminute absque tantummodo peccato significata." The Copts had no need, therefore, to renounce the *formula* of Saint Cyril in order to be restored to full communion with the Roman Church, but only to interpret this formula in a restricted sense. On these problems, which have been given renewed attention recently, cf. the contributions

of Heyer, Karmiris, Nersoyan, in *Monde non crétien,* 77 (1966), 3-56; and of Msgr. Emilianos (*Lutheran World,* Saint Louis, 1966). In the light of Lateran, 649, and of Saint Martin I, long after Chalcedon, it does not seem exact to write, as does Father Guérard des Lauriers: "we no longer say that Christ possesses one nature." We should rather write that we no longer say *only* that. An important ecumenical problem is involved.

13. See the end of the preceding note.

14. Father G. des Lauriers O.P., cited by Father Le Guillou; cf. note 11. Father des Lauriers rightly stresses that, while there are two *operations* in the incarnate Word, there is in Him only one *operant.* This is what Saint Cyril had profoundly grasped. The Dominican theologian also introduces an idea which is very true: Christ as man enjoys the beatifying vision of the eternal breathing of the Spirit, through His own divine Person as the Word, but He cannot entitatively share in it as man. In this connection, see the fine interpretation of Saint John of the Cross (*Living Flame,* str. 4, verses 4-6) given by J. Maritain, *Les Degés du Savoir,* chap. IX, par. 15, Paris, 1959⁶, .pages 749-753. Finally, in answer to Father des Lauriers' profound reflections on the unity of the *esse* of Christ as an explanation of the exactitude of Saint Cyril's intuition ("a reality one and incarnate"), one could not put forward the famous text of Saint Thomas Aquinas concerning the "esse secundarium" of Christ as man, because Maritain also very clearly shows (*ibid.,* pp. 868-872) that, according to the same Saint Thomas, there is only one *esse personale* in Christ, the *esse secundarium* being merely a temporal and created *esse* proper to human nature. Cf. Saint Thomas Aquinas, *de Unione Verbi incarnati,* 4. 1. Through the *esse secundarium,* the Person of the Word exists, not purely and simply, but humanly.

15. Cf. Jn. 7, 39; on this point, see F. X. Durwell C.SS.R., *La Résurrection de Jésus, Mystère de Salut,* Paris, 1961⁶, pp. 102-110.

16. H. M. Diepen O.S.B., "L'Esprit du Coeur de Jésus," *Cor Jesu,* Rome, 1959, I, 188.

17. Pius XII, *Haurietis Aquas,* AAS, 48 (1959) 335: note that "ejus" refers to "cordis" and not merely to "Jesus." In this connection, let us note the following fine commentary by Father Diepen: "The eternal procession of the Third Person, immanent end of the Love of the Father and of the Son, is the principal idea in the phrase which already surprises us much less than at first sight: the Spirit of the Heart of Jesus." (*op. cit.,* I, 173). The Spirit is *of* the Heart of Jesus because of the threefold love of Christ, but especially because of His divine love.

18. It is well known that the encyclical has set aside the

Vulgate punctuation and adopted that suggested by recent exegetical and patristic studies (cf. H. Rahner, S.J., *Biblica,* 22, 1941, pp. 269-302; the article is entitled "Flumina de ventre Christi"). Nevertheless, it is not entirely exact to write (Diepen, *op. cit.,* I, 152) that the Scriptural citation indicated by Jn. 7, 38, cannot be found in the Old Testament if one accepts the Vulgate punctuation and if one supposes that the "rivers of living water" flow from the "belly" of the believer: Is. 58, 11 would suffice to justify Jn. 7, 38; but it must be recognized that the believer, not his "belly," is presented by this text as a spring "of living water." Anyhow, Jn. 7, 38, should be read in the light of Jn. 4, 14: the Heart of Jesus is "a spring of water" which makes the believer, in its likeness, a derivative source.

19. Here is the Latin text on this important point: "ipse (Jesus) 'aquae vivae' fontem pollicebatur *e suo sinu oriturum.*" The italics are ours. Cf. note 20.

20. Pius XII, *Haurietis Aquas,* 48 (1956), 310. From Jn. 7, 38-39, as properly understood by Tradition and by the magisterium (Pius XII), it emerges therefore that Christ Himself invites us to drink the Spirit flowing from His pierced Heart (cf. Jn. 19, 37), to venerate His wounds (cf. 20, 27), and especially the wound in His side. The public Revelation, understood and interpreted by Saint John, already showed Christ's desire to see His Heart an object of adoring worship, at least an implicit desire for this. Up to now, it seems, what we state here has not been made the subject of an analytical study, or even of an effort of precise focus.

21. Pius XII, *Haurietis Aquas,* AAS, 48 (1956), 320. The arid and dried up soil of sinful humanity becomes, thanks to the baptismal water which flows from the Heart of Christ, the paradise of the holy Church.

22. *Ibid.,* par. 24 (AAS, 48, 1956, 323).

23. Diepen, *op. cit.,* I, 189.

24. In giving the Spirit, the Heart (divine or human) does not relinquish Him; for the Spirit is present in the Son by virtue of the mystery of circuminsession, and He dwells in the human soul of the incarnate Word.

25. Diepen, *op. cit.,* I, 185-186. Dom Diepen here probes in an original way the traditional doctrine of the visible mission of the Spirit. The Council (AG, 4) has taken up the traditional doctrine of Saint Leo the Great and of Leo XIII: "Doubtless, the Holy Spirit was already at work in the world before Christ was glorified; but, on the day of Pentecost, He came down upon the disciples . . . and the gospel began to spread upon the nations . . ." (Abbott, pp. 587-588). Dom Diepen has shown convincingly that this visible mission of the Spirit not only signifies that He was poured forth more abundantly in a quantitative sense, but also implies a quali-

tatively new doctrinal nuance of love; cf. 1 Jn. 2, 20-21. 27; 1 Cor. 2, 11-16.

26. Cf. PO, 5. 2.

27. Cf. LG, 23.1; 26. 1.

28. An interpretation dear to Saint John Chrysostom. Cf. J. Lecuyer, *Le sacrifice de la Nouvelle Alliance,* Lyon, 1962, p. 262; PG, 61, 251 (*In* 1 *Cor., Hom.* 30, 2).

29. Saint John Damascene, *De fide orthodoxa,* IV. 13. PG, 94, 1149.

30. Scheeben, *The Mysteries of Christianity,* St. Louis, 1958, V, chap. 18, par. 75. We give extracts from this in an appendix. To mark the importance of this theme, let it suffice to recall here, with Scheeben, the ancient custom of reserving the Blessed Sacrament in a "peristerium" or ciborium in the form of a dove, symbol of the Spirit who gives the Eucharist.

31. Desire, inspired by the Spirit, to eat the spiritualized flesh of Christ, and to receive the Holy Spirit through the Body of Christ. Cf. DS, 1648 (DB, 881).

32. In citing these texts, we are of course aware that 1 Cor. 15, 44 uses the Greek word "soma," whereas the Johannine texts use the word "sarx." But this point is secondary to our line of thought here.

33. Saint Thomas Aquinas, *Summa Theologica,* I. 39. 7; *de Veritate,* 7. 3.

34. GS, 38. 1. (Abbott, 236).

35. Cf. note 20 of this chapter.

36. The author is not using the word in the technical sense, reserved to the Bible, of which however there is question in the preceding words. It would be more accurate to speak of assistance.

37. H. Holstein S.J., in a work edited by H. du Manoir S.J., *Maria* (Paris, 1961, t. VI, p. 290). Notice on this occasion the complexity of the basis of the worship due to the Sacred Heart of Jesus: on the one hand, the encyclical, *Haurietis Aquas,* presents this Heart as "the most impressive *natural* symbol of the love which the divine Redeemer continues to feel for the human race" (par. 50; Latin text, p. 341); on the other hand, it shows in "*Scripture and Tradition* the profound source of this devotion" (par. 64; Latin text, p. 341). It presupposes, therefore, that right reason, concretely enlightened by grace, recognizes, in the midst of a correct anthropological vision, the "natural symbolism" of the heart. One may hold that here too Revelation has been the occasion, not to say the cause, of an anthropological deepening, as in the case of the Augustinian considerations on the trinitarian structure of the human soul, created in the image of the living God.

38. Cf. A. Hamon S.J., *Histoire de la Dévotion au Sacré-Coeur,* Paris, 1940, t. V, p. 248.

39. Cf. A. Rayez and A. de Bonhomme, DSAM, IV 2, art.

"Eucharistique (Coeur)," col. 1651, published in 1961. On the one measure which still exists, see our chapter XIV, note 27.

40. This feast has been suppressed in the course of the liturgical reform. See Chap. I, note 12.

41. Pius XII, *Haurietis Aquas,* par. 82; AAS, 48 (1956), 351: "Nec facile percipere erit vim amoris, quo Christus compulsus nobis se ipse exhibuit spirituale alimentum, nisi peculiari modo Eucharistici Cordis Jesu cultum fovendo."

42. Declaration of the Holy Office, 27 May 1891, cited by Rayez and Bonhomme, DSAM, IV. 2, (1961) col. 1651, art. "Eucharistique (Coeur)." We note that, nevertheless, the declaration of Leo XIII in 1901 and that of Pius XII in 1956 (citing, however, his predecessor) have shifted the ground of the problem, because the Eucharistic Heart is not purely and simply identical with the Sacred Heart in the Eucharist, since the first expression also connotes the past decision which led to the loving institution of the Holy Eucharist. In this connection, it would not be wrong to say that the devotion to the Sacred Heart is, in a sense, more perfect than that of the Eucharist.

43. An expression of J. Jacques S.C.J., in "Culte et Théologie du Sacré-Coeur," *Année Théologique,* 8 (1947), 274; cited by Father Hartman S.C.J., *Le sens plénier de la réparation du péché,* Louvain, 1955, pp. 254-255. Although Vatican II (LG, 51) speaks of "the authentic cult of the saints" (Abbott, p. 84), the word *cult* is generally used with a more clearly theological meaning than the word "devotion." The saints have a right only to "dulia," the Sacred Heart to a cult of "latria" or adoration.

44. Saint Cyril of Alexandria, in Jo. 11, 10; PG. 74, 545. See E. Mersch S.J., *Le Corps Mystique du Christ,* Paris, 1951³, t. I. p. 520.

45. Saint Cyril of Alexandria, *in Jo.,* V, 2; PG, 73, 753-756; cf. Mersch, *op. cit.,* p. 515.

46. Cyril, *in Jo.* 11, 12; PG, 74, 564-565; cf. Mersch, *op. cit.,* pp. 508-509.

47. Cf. however PG, 76, 1163 B.

48. In his commentary on Jn. 20, 22 (PG, 74, 710; cf. 76, 1188), Saint Cyril, not without reason, says that the action of the Risen Christ, in symbolizing by His breathing on the disciples the gift of His Holy Spirit to them, signifies that the Spirit proceeds from the Father through the Son. He very clearly implies (PG, 76, 1188) that the flesh of Christ gives the Spirit. See S. Tromp, *De Christo Capite,* Rome, 1960, pp. 215-226.

49. Cf. Saint Irenaeus, *Adversus Haereses,* III. 18. 3; PL, 7, 234: "In Christi enim nomine subauditur qui unxit et ipse

qui unctus est et ipsa unctio in qua unctus est. Et unxit quidem Pater, unctus est vero Filius, in Spiritu qui est unctio."

50. Cf. chap. XIV, D.

51. In a direct way, the Heart of Jesus symbolizes the human and divine love of the incarnate Word; indirectly, It symbolizes the love of the Father and of the Son, which love is the principle of the human love of the incarnate Word.

52. Pius XII, *Haurietis Aquas,* par. 49 (Latin text, p. 335: "mutuus amor Personalis Patris erga Filium et Filii erga Patrem").

53. *Ibid.,* par. 54 (Latin text, p. 338).

54. Cf. J. Guillet S.J., DSAM, IV, 2 (1961), col. 1246-1247: art. *"Esprit-Saint dans l'Ecriture."*

55. We are here closely following M. J. Scheeben, *The Mysteries of Christianity,* St. Louis, 1958, pp. 60-65, chap. II, par. 10, pp. 59, 63-64. His explanation could be correlated with those of Saint Thomas Aquinas (*Summa con. Gen.,* IV, chap. 23, par. 1; or par. 3592 of the Marietti Edition, Rome, 1961): "nomen spiritus a respiratione animalium sumptum videtur in qua aer cum quodam motu infertur et emittitur. Unde nomen spiritus ad omnem impulsum et motum vel cujuscumque aeri corporis trahitur et sic ventus dicitur spiritus. . . . Quia aer invisibilis est, translatum est ulterius spiritus nomen ad omnes virtutes et substantias invisibiles et motivas. Et propter hoc et anima sensibilis et angeli et Deus spiritus dicuntur; et proprie Deus per modum amoris procedens quia amor virtutem quandam motivam insinuat" (Book IV, chap. 23, par. 1—or par. 3592 of the Marietti edition, Rome, 1961). The text is enlightening. Saint Thomas clearly understood the original connection between the term "Holy Breath" which Jesus uses to describe the Third Person of the Trinity, and the word "breath" as applied to animal respiration. He thus opens the way to a more clearly anthropological understanding of this term: the animal breath in accordance with which the Holy Spirit is so designated, is a human breath, because man is the animal *par excellence* who understands the other animals by reference to himself. The Old Testament describes the wind as the "breath from the nostrils of Yahweh" (Ex. 15, 8) seen in terms of a man who breathes: it is with this in mind that we must understand the expression "Breath (or Spirit) of God," and therefore the expression "Holy Spirit" in the New Testament. We can thus more readily understand how Jesus could refer to the Spirit as His Holy Breath, and why He willed to give It by breathing on His disciples, since Jesus knows Himself to be God equal to the Father. On the meaning of the word "Spirit" (Ruah), see Ceuppens O.P., *Theologia biblica,* t. II, Rome, 1949, p. 48 *seq.* The connection which Saint Thomas made between animal breath, analogously affirmed of God, and affective and loving impulses, and pulsa-

tions, is itself not without foundation in the New Testament (cf. 1 Cor. 4, 2; 6, 17; 11 Cor. 12, 18; Eph. 4, 3; Phil. 1, 27); we thank Father P. B. Kipper S.J. who pointed out this fact to us. It is not surprising, therefore, that the mode in which the risen Christ gave the Spirit, His Holy Breath—and, with the Spirit, the power to forgive sins—was that of the exhalation that is part of the process of breathing.

56. Cf. Father Congar's remark quoted in Chapter Ten, note 8.

57. In the context of the citations given in note 55, it will be noticed that, just before breathing on His disciples in giving them the Spirit, Jesus showed them the open wound in His side, a source of great joy for them (Jn. 20, 20-22). The Evangelist thus implies anew (cf. Jn. 7, 39; 19, 34-37) that the Spirit is a gift of the pierced Heart of the glorified Christ; and, we remark in passing, that the disciples, on the very day of the Resurrection, see with joy Him whom they have pierced (identical Greek verb used in Jn. 19, 37, and 20, 20). Above all, in clearly affirming the connection between the gift of the Divine Breath and the Risen Christ's exhaling of the breath He has resumed (cf. Jn. 19, 30, and 20, 22), the Evangelist gives us to understand that all his other statements concerning the Holy Spirit must be understood in the light of this manifestation of the glorious Christ. The Holy Spirit is the Breath sent by Jesus as Word and given by Him as Word made flesh, because, in dying, He has delivered up to the Father His purely human breath.

58. Saint Augustine says, on the one hand, that the Holy Spirit is "communio" between the Father and the Son (*in Jo. tract.,* 105) and, on the other, that He is "caritas substantialis et consubstantialis amborum" (*in Jo. tract.,* 105, 3; PL, 1904 d).

59. The Eucharistic species, on the one hand, and the Eucharistic Communion of the faithful, on the other, are, properly speaking, the visible sign of the unity of the Spirit (the species being considered from the viewpoint of the breaking of one and the same consecrated bread). The visibility of the Eucharistic Heart supposes the mediation of the "eyes of faith" (cf. Eph. 1, 18), just as today the "visibility" of the Heart of Jesus supposes it. This sign comes into the category of the "prophecy" intelligible to the unbeliever or the uninitiated through a mystagogy (cf. 1 Cor. 14, 22-25) which unveils in this Eucharistic Heart the present and active sign of the whole Christian mystery and of the "pleroma." It is precisely this which constitutes its superiority as sign in relation to the already very rich significance of the Heart of Jesus, a sign which does not accentuate in the same way (though it too accentuates) the real and actual presence among us of Christ and of His loving sacrifice, as the nucleus of the whole synthesis (real and logically established) of the Christian

mystery. It could be said that the Eucharistic Heart of Jesus is preeminently the "totalizing sign" of this mystery. It combines the purely anthropological sign of *heart* with the cosmo-anthropological sign of *bread and wine*. In isolating one aspect of what It signifies (cf. chap. 14, texts cited in notes 29 and 30) and in having a more particular object, this Eucharistic Heart more clearly manifests the totality of the pleroma, and consequently its value in preaching the Gospel is greater (cf. note 42 of this chapter).

60. Cf., e.g., Saint Fulgence de Ruspe: PL, 65, 184-192; 788-791; 769; 812.

61. Latin text of the third Eucharistic anaphora ("concede, ut qui Corpore et Sanguine Filii tui reficimur, Spiritu ejus Sancto repleti, unum corpus et unus spiritus inveniamur in Christo") published on 23 May 1968.

62. One understands, therefore, how Saint John Chrysostom could say that the Eucharist is the breast of the mystery of the Spirit—a breast at which, like children, we drink the grace of the Spirit (quoted by Scheeben, *The Mysteries of Christianity*, V, XVIII, par 75, note 19): "hom. de S. Philogonio."

63. Cf. the text of Pius XII cited in note 20 of this chapter.

64. Letter addressed by Paul VI to the superiors general of the religious institutes vowed to the cult of the Sacred Heart (25 May 1965). This letter does not appear to have been published by AAS, but it is contained in the *Actes Pontificaux* of Paul VI, no. 148 (Bellarmin, Montreal).

65. Cardinal Amette, *Revue de l'Adoration Réparatrice*, 1903, p. 138; cited by R. Brouillard, encyclopedia *Catholicisme*, 1949, t. II, col. 1282 (art. "Coeur Euch.").

66. Cf. Chapter Fourteen, note 30.

67. Cf. note 41 of this chapter.

3

THE DEVELOPMENT OF HUMANITY
AND THE SACRIFICE OF CHRIST

We have seen how Christ unites Himself with the
Church through the Eucharist and in the Holy Spirit.
Like its invisible Head, this Church is "for the life
of the world." It ceaselessly associates itself with the
work of Christ. However, the world of which, thanks
to Him, the Church is the coredeemer, is a world in
evolution, in growth. What is the relationship between
this development and the sacrifice of the Church in the
Eucharist mystery? How are we to understand the
idea and the reality of this development at its different
levels? In answering these questions, in inverse order,
we shall have occasion to sum up the results of our
inquiry into the mystery of Christ the Redeemer, or
at least some of these results. This will logically lead
to a statement of the absolute need for an existential
decision in favor of the Redeemer and of the coredemptive activity, the basic and obligatory vocation of every
human person. We mean the decision concerning human and Eucharistic development.

90

A. The Development of Man, of Humanity, and of the Church

By his encyclical *Populorum Progressio* ("On Fostering the Development of Peoples"), Paul VI has certainly helped the Church to a better understanding both of the importance and of the meaning of development. He has thus opened up new paths to theological reflection on earthly matters, on the historicity of man, and on humanism.

In gathering together the scattered data which this encyclical offers us concerning development, we begin with the following idea:

> In order to be authentic, development must be complete, integral; that is, it must promote the good of every man and of the whole man. . . . In the design of God, every man is called upon to develop and fulfill himself, for every life is a vocation. At birth, everyone is granted, in germ, a set of aptitudes and qualities for him to bring to fruition. This coming to maturity, which will be the result of education received from the environmental and personal efforts, will allow each man to direct himself towards the destiny intended for him by his Creator. Endowed with intelligence and freedom, he is responsible for his fulfillment as he is for his salvation. He is aided, or sometimes impeded, by those who educate him and those with whom he lives, but each one remains, whatever be these influences affecting him, the principal agent of his own success or failure. By the unaided[1] effort of his own intelligence and will, each man can grow in humanity, can enhance his personal worth, can become more a person.[2]

Development is, therefore, something which reaches well beyond any considerations of economic demands or productivity. It is essentially a person's vocation to human growth; it is therefore a mission, a responsibility, a duty. Each will have to account to God for his success or his failure. Man is not born fully de-

veloped, but born with a mission to achieve his own
fulness. "As Pascal has said so well: 'Man infinitely
surpasses man.' "[3]   In other words, the inner man
developed to his full personal potential should be regarded as the masterpiece of mankind.

It is to every human person, considered in the concrete fullness of his nature as aided by grace, that the
parable of the talents applies. Each receives, as his
initial capital, natural and supernatural, a "set of
aptitudes and qualities for him to bring to fruition"
through "the education received from the environmental and personal effort,"[4] these being the conditions
for the success of the project of man and of the plan
of God.

Such a vision of man as bound in conscience to be
the architect of his own development, links up, while
surpassing and extending it, with what Stalin said on
4 May 1936: "Man is the most valuable capital."
Paul VI shows us that no man is deprived, at birth,
of his capital of *humanity* without which all other
capital would be useless, and with which—despite deficiencies as regards economic resources or instruction,
and even if "impeded by those who educate him and
those with whom he lives"[5]—every man can reach
those inseparable degrees of human growth and of
supernatural holiness to which Providence càlls him.

It emerges clearly, therefore, that socio-economic
underdevelopment cannot prevent any individual from
realizing his human and spiritual betterment. Man is
never the slave of his environment. Inseparably a social, rational, and religious animal as he is, his freedom is not and cannot be suppressed by others. Every
man remains always free to become more a man.

On the basis of such a conviction, it is easier to promote a "true humanism . . which is open to the Absolute," and consequently to secure "the fully-rounded
development of the whole man and of all men."[6]
This "new humanism" cannot be cut away from "the
higher values of love and friendship, of prayer and
contemplation."[7]   For is it not in prayer and contem-

plation that man finds the strength to love his fellowmen, and the freedom to grow humanly and spiritually despite environmental obstacles?

To every man, grace offers this invitation to liberating prayer; for in himself every man is "open to the Absolute," and therefore capable of growth, of development, of humanization. Grace can also "open to" the transcendent Absolute, and therefore introduce to full humanism even those who deliberately close themselves against the Absolute which is inviting them. Should it not be said that it belongs to efficacious grace to open gently to the Absolute those who, not without doing violence to the most profound aspirations of their nature, have closed themselves against it? Needless to say, such grace would in no way violate their human freedom of choice.

In the light of the Biblical and Catholic doctrine of supernatural elevation and of efficacious grace, one already grasps more readily the content and the significance of "transcendent humanism."[8] Man cannot be fully man without the grace which divinizes him; for, in divinizing, grace humanizes. A man who, rejecting the idea of divinizing help, sought to be "man and more than man," would fall to a sub-human level.

In "transcendent humanism," therefore, we have a real fusion—but without confusion of identity—of the growth, humanization, and divinization of the human person. Integral development is identical with full and transcendent humanism; this twofold reality supposes, however, an inner tension in him who lives it. What man, tempted by his evil inclinations, has not experienced to what extent "the exclusive pursuit of possessions becomes an obstacle to individual fulfillment and to man's true greatness"?[9]

In order "to be more," it is often necessary to fight against the selfish desire to have more, in order that others may "have more" and "be more." Often, richness of being presupposes poverty of actual, and especially of desired, possessions. More precisely, the efficaciousness of my desire to have more for others, will often be linked with the mortification of my greed to have more for myself. "For you know the grace of our Lord Jesus Christ, that though he was rich, yet for your sake he became poor, so that by his poverty you might become rich," writes Saint Paul (2 Cor. 8, 9).

Already, from this viewpoint, one can weigh and consider a truth to which we shall return: namely, that there is no development, no growth of man and of humanity, without sacrifice. "Being more" sometimes demands "having more," but more often it demands "having less."[10]

The same sacrificial tension is found in Saint Paul. On the one hand, as we have seen, he presents Christ as increasing our being by Himself having less; on the other hand, he invites Christians "to grow up in every way into him who is the head, into Christ" (Eph. 4, 15), and he prays that the Colossians "may abound more and more, with knowledge and all discernment" (Col. 1, 9). On behalf of the Christians of Philippi, he gives us the perfect prayer of earthly development polarized by an eschatological vision:

> And it is my prayer that your love may abound more and more, with knowledge and all discernment, so that you may approve what is excellent, and may be pure and blameless, for the day of Christ, filled with the fruits of righteousness which come through Jesus Christ, to the glory and praise of God (Phil. 1, 9-11).

In these Pauline texts, one sees how the Revelation of the Mystery of Christ sharpens and makes sublime the natural desire of man in any age, which Paul VI sums up in the qualities relevant to our own times: "in brief, to seek to do more, know more, and have more in order to be more."[11] Is there not a divinization of *doing* in the works of charity, of *knowing* in faith, of *having* in the hope that anticipates possession, of *being* in the grace inseparable from charity? Could one separate the aspiration to full earthly development and the thirst for a permanent divinization? Can one talk about the first, but remain silent about the second?

In no circumstances, however, must this necessary eschatological insistence be taken as a warrant to diminish the earthly aspect of development, for which, in reality, it provides both basis and encouragement. With development integrally considered, underdevelopment is contrasted in both its material and its moral aspecs: 'the lack of material necessities for those who are without the minimum essential for life; the moral deficiencies of those who are mutilitated by selfishness."[12]

In the midst of the integral vision of transcendent humanism, it is clear that the worst underdevelopment is not that of the victims of "undeserved misery," but much more that of men who mutilate their own humanity by exploiting the misery of others. The moral underdevelopment of the economically developed nations could reduce their *being* in inverse ratio to the increase of their *having*.

Far removed from all philosophical idealism and from empty pretension to consider the soul in complete abstraction from the body and from society, the very idea of development here recalled in the light of the teaching of Paul VI implies the physical side of man who aspires to "subsistence, health and fixed employment,"[13] and who ought so to aspire, not only for himself, but also for others.

A Christian and integral vision of development overcomes, therefore, the twofold danger of dualist Platonism and of monist materialism: the first would claim to be interested only in spiritual growth; the second, only in economic growth. The Christian vision looks to "the fully-rounded development of the whole man and of all men."

Society today has collective duties towards the society of the future. An exclusive pursuit of possessions on our part, could injure the specifically human quality of generations to come. The inner tension already mentioned is accompanied by an historical tension.

The Church, composed as it is of people belonging to different generations, encounters through them the same tensions. "Sharing the noblest aspirations of men and suffering when she sees them not satisfied, the Church wishes to help them to attain their full flowering, and that is why she offers men what she possesses as her characteristic attribute: a global vision of man and of the human race."[14]

If the Church wishes to help men to attain their full flowering, is not this because through that flowering the Church yearns to achieve its own fullness? Is not the pilgrim Church a Church in process of development, a Church with an obligation to grow in numbers and in quality? Is it not "the body that upbuilds itself in love," by laboring to "grow up in every way into him who is the head, into Christ"? If it organizes its "saints, for the work of ministry, for building up the body of Christ," is not this because at the end we must all come together "to build up together that perfect Man of whom Saint Paul speaks 'who realizes the fullness of Christ' " (Eph. 4, 12-16).[15]

The intense interest which the Church takes in development can be fully understood only in the light of an ever greater awareness that it has itself a duty to grow for the glory of its Head. It too, at its own supernatural level, wishes and must wish "to do more, to know more, and to have more in order to be more" until it finally reaches its fullness on the last day of its earthly history.

The development of mankind and even that of each individual person involve the growth of the Church— although, of course, the Church is not to be confused with humanity, or any of its members, or any man. Pauline ecclesiology, especially in the Epistle to the Ephesians, is an ecclesiology of development. This is not surprising; for, is not Paul's missionary companion, Saint Luke, the evangelist of the growth of Christ as well as being the historian of the growth in numbers and quality of the Church whose infancy (still continuing as long as history endures) imitates that of its Master?

Let us recall, substituting the present tense for the

past,[16] the principal texts of Saint Luke about the growth of the Church and of Christ: "And the word of God increases; and the number of the disciples greatly. . . . So the word of the Lord grows and prevails mightily" (Acts 6, 7; 19, 20). Such growth of the Church, the Body of Christ, in the course of its pilgrimage, signifies in the final analysis that Christ grows through it. Incomplete, in a sense, He grows towards His full eschatological stature: "And the child grows and becomes strong filled with wisdom; and the favor of God is upon him. . . . And Jesus increases in wisdom and in stature, and in favor with God and man" (Lk. 2, 40. 52: changed to present tense). Does not Saint Luke take pleasure in describing the growth of the historic Christ in order to underline its mystical and ecclesial extension in human history?

Is it not from its own continual growth that the Church is particularly able to grasp and promote the integral development of man and of humanity, that is to say, the growth of Christ in them?

It might be objected, however, that the history of the Church is not one of unbroken progress, but one marked at times by setbacks. At a certain level of events, this cannot be denied. But these setbacks provide the matter and the occasion for an invisible progress in depth. By accepting the permissive will of God concerning apostasies, heresies, schisms, the Church progresses in submission to the Redeemer. This explains why Vatican II could very clearly declare: "Seeking after the glory of Christ, the Church becomes more like her exalted model, and continually progresses in faith, hope, and charity, searching out and doing the will of God in all things."[17]

A Church which proclaims its continual progress in its most intimate and most essential activity, is a Church always unsatisfied with the degree of growth to which it has already attained. For it, growth is a duty recognized as such. Consequently, is not the Church particularly fitted to present to the world the obligation of integral development? Who could refuse to a Church in constant and humble growth, the right to invite men to become one with its own development, in the progress of its faith, its hope, and its charity?

One must even carry the matter further by saying, not only that the Church works its own growth through human development insofar as the latter signifies a transcendent humanism, but also that the aspect of earthly progress involved in this development is of great importance for the growth of Christ, though they remain distinct.[18]

Since the idea of development is greater than that of earthly progress, it can be said that the growth of the reign of Christ, which transcends the latter, does not transcend the former.

This amounts to affirming, both of the development with which *Populorum Progressio* is concerned and of the growth of the reign of the Redeemer, that we can say with Saint Paul:

> I planted, Apollos watered, but God gave the growth. So neither he who plants nor he who waters is anything, but only God who gives the growth. He who plants and he who waters are equal, and each shall receive his wages according to his labor. For we are fellow workers for God; you are God's field, God's building (1 Cor. 3, 6-9).

Through the secondary causes, the first Cause and supreme author of development is God, the Father of Our Lord Jesus Christ. The growth of man is the work of the Father, his Creator. Not only does He call man to *self-development* as an obligation in conscience, but by watering with the water of His Spirit the "branches" of Jesus, "the true Vine," the Father who is "the vinedresser" develops them and causes them to bear fruit (cf. Jn. 15, 1-4). The work of development, undertaken in Christ, deserves wages because it constitutes a cooperation with God. It is the Father who, with His two hands, the Son and the Spirit,[19] enables man to "do more, to know more, and to have more, in order to be more."

The words of Jesus, "Apart from me you can do nothing" (Jn. 15, 5), also apply to integral development. Without Christ's grace, there is no fully human development.

This is not surprising, since development is synonymous with growth of the extensions of Christ's humanity. But, just as Christ had to pass by means of death from the "less human conditions" of His pre-paschal life to the "more human conditions" of His life as the Risen Lord, so too man will achieve self-development only by passing through self-abnegation, through uniting himself with the Pasch of the Redeemer.

B. Development and Eucharistic Sacrifice

A Christian vision of the development presupposes reflection on death, which is its means *par excellence*.

This statement may at first sight seem a complete paradox, for is not death the definitive negation of all growth and of all progress? How can it be said that it is the means *par excellence* of development?

It suffices to remind ourselves, however, in the light of the dead and risen Christ, that death is the condition and the price of the final and definitive blossoming of that "set of aptitutes and qualities" which every man received "at birth," if we may use the already quoted words of Paul VI.[20] How can one forget the answer of Jesus: "Truly, truly, I say to you, unless a grain of wheat falls into the earth and dies, it remains alone; but if it dies, it bears much fruit" (Jn. 12, 24)? Without the resurrection of the body, there is no enduring growth, no definitive development.

Is not the resurrection of the body, together with the beatific vision granted to souls, the development *par excellence* which Christ brings to the world? Without and prior to this resurrection, where is one to find the perfection of "being more" to which man aspires? Are not all the other desires polarized by a natural desire to conquer death and to see God?[21]

The acceptance of death is linked, therefore, with the desire of the human person for self-growth and self-blossoming. In *Populorum Progressio*, Paul VI implicitly noted this fact: "This road towards a greater humanity requires effort and sacrifice; but suffering itself, accepted for the love of our brethren, favors the progress of the entire human family. Christians know that union with the sacrifice of our Savior contributes to the building up of the Body of God in its plenitude: the assembled People of God."[22]

In the Eucharistic sacrifice, we see the harmonizing of the acceptance of death and of the fight for life and for survival, on earth and beyond the earth, personal and collective.

I can offer the death of Christ and my own death only "for the life of the world" (Jn. 6, 51). "And he died for all, that those who live might live no longer for themselves but for him who for their sake died and was raised" (2 Cor. 5, 15).

To participate in the Mass, to receive Communion, is not this to signify publicly a constantly renewed engagement to work for the peace, the growth, the development of men?—and all this for the glory of Christ who has died and risen from the dead for their sake?

The Eucharist is the sacrament of fraternal love: it signifies and effects this love in the communicants. "By this we know love, that he laid down his life for us; and we ought to lay down our lives for the brethren. But if anyone has the world's goods and sees his brother in need, yet closes his heart against him, how does God's love abide in him?" (1 Jn. 3, 16-17).

Through the Eucharist, Christ abides in him who receives It. Christ enters into him in order to love other men with a sacrificial love; He opens the heart of him who eats His flesh and drinks His blood. Through Communion, Christ effects the temporal and salvific engagement of the Christian, but without confining Himself to signifying it.

It is thus that the Eucharist, sacrament of perseverance in fraternal love and in involvement with other men's temporal development, shows itself to be the efficacious sign of the very goal of human growth—

namely, the glorious resurrection. "He who eats my flesh and drinks my blood has eternal life, and I will raise him up at the last day" (Jn. 6, 54).

One gathers from this that Christ has specially emphasized, not the temporal or purely individual aspect of human development, but its eternal and social mystery: "Do not labor for the food which perishes, but for the food which endures to eternal life, which the Son of man will give to you; for on him has God the Father set his seal" (Jn. 6, 27)—i.e. the seal of His Holy Spirit.[23] Is not the Eucharist this food? And should not the Christian labor to nourish Christ who is hungry in men (cf. Mt. 25, 35-40), and hungry to grow in them through the Eucharist?

The Eucharist, therefore, assumes the aspect of the sacrament of integral human development.

As such, it becomes the immediate end of the In-humanation of the Word. By inserting Himself as the Word Incarnate into human society in order to unite and recapitulate mankind in Himself, the Word became the promoter of the development of man, such development being the *raison d'être* of His Incarnation.

Having come "that they may have life, and have it abundantly" (Jn. 10, 10), the Lord Jesus, through the efforts of His members to promote the development of each and every man, wills to lead the pre-Christians to recognize Him, in the Eucharist, as their salvation and their life.

The dialogue for and about development thus globally considered, becomes an integral part of the dialogue of salvation for which the Word was made human word and transubstantiating word.

In the heart of this development, the cosmos becomes transfigured, as Christ, through the Eucharist, increasingly assumes the world and human history. In this way, the best of the Teilhardian vision is realized.

Through His own existential choice of a redemptive death, a decision clearly manifested at the Last Supper, Christ merited, founded, and polarized the existential decision of the Christian. This latter decision, far from being that of a faith almost devoid of content, as Bultmann supposes, is a decision to opt for human and divine growth. We shall return shortly to this point.

As the Word whose language condemns the deceitful word of men,[25] the anti-logos Logos, Christ is therefore precisely the man-for-others, the man devoted in an exemplary way to the full growth of all the others, for the glory of the Father. In proportion as, following Christ's example, he sacrifices himself for the growth of his brethren, the Christian becomes with Christ, as Bonhoeffer would have him to be, a "man-for-others."

Preeminently, it is Christ Himself, in His Eucharist, who makes the Christian a "man-for-others." In consecrating him to Himself, he "transsecularizes" him and makes him pass with Himself to the Father, in the same act by which the Christian engages himself to live, not for himself, but for others and for Christ-in-the-others.

Christ, author and consummator of this development, is the Prophet of the growth of humanity, its Priest and its Victim, its Recapitulator. He redeems His Church to the point of making it the coredemptrix of the world's growth. For the same purpose, He extends through and in the Church, His sacrificial celibacy and His primacy of love.

The Eucharistic Heart of Jesus is, therefore, through His Spirit, the active nucleus of human development.

The growth of the world is dependent on the sacrifice of the Lamb, even if the existence of the universe is not dependent on that sacrifice.[26]

Thus it emerges that all the themes developed in this book converge on and meet in the Eucharist, sacrifice and sacrament of human development.

The Eucharist is the sacrifice of human development in the sense that in it Christ offers His life to the Father for the supernatural success of the human enterprise at whose head He has placed Himself. Consequently, it is the whole human universe, even at the natural level, that benefits from the bloody sacrifice of the Redeemer.

The Eucharist is also the sacrifice of the development *in* love, just as it is the efficacious sign of the growth *of* love in this world. It signifies and effects the passage from less human to more human conditions. It does so by promoting and vivifying the twofold existential decision of the Christian who aims to labor at the construction of the earthly city while at the same time he seeks to become increasingly one flesh and one victim with Christ, our Pasch, through frequent Communion.

C. The Existential Decision of Human Development

If "human fulfillment constitutes, as it were, a summary of our duties,"[27] it should be made the object of a free, deliberate, and constantly renewed choice.

The decision to seek self-fulfillment and to help others to fulfill themselves for the glory of God, is the concrete expression of the love of the heavenly Father and of one's brethren. In this connection, Bultmann's idea holds good: "The worth of a man is not determined by his human quality . . . but simply by the decision he makes in the here-and-now of his present life."[28]

Faced with the increasing gap between the developed and the under-developed countries, faced with the hunger, ignorance, and misery of innumerable people, should not each ask himself the questions put by Paul VI: "Is he prepared to support out of his own pocket works and undertakings organized in favor of the most destitute? Is he ready to pay higher taxes so that the public authorities can intensify their efforts in favor of development? Is he ready to pay a higher price for imported goods so that the producer may be more justly rewarded? Or to leave his country, if necessary and if he is young, in order to assist in this development of the young nations?"[29] In short, is he prepared to assist in "building a world where every man, no matter what his race, religion, or nationality, can live a fully human life"?[30]

To devote oneself to development is to opt for a

hard, personal poverty directed to the improvement of the lot of others.

When the Christian accepts the obligation to promote development, he works at one and the same time for the building up of the world and for the building up of the Church, because the growth of man and the growth of the Church go hand in hand, as we have shown in the early part of this chapter.

When one has properly grasped that the Eucharist is characterized by a dynamism of love, it becomes clear that frequent reception of this "sacrament of development" is the supreme mediate factor which decides the temporal efficaciousness of our engagement.[31]

This latter especially needs the fire of charity, whose nucleus is communion with the Eucharistic Heart of Jesus.

Is it not through eating the flesh and drinking the blood of the immolated and triumphant Lamb that the Christian will find the strength to immolate himself with Him to the Father, for the development of others? How could he himself grow without the Eucharist?

To be fully efficacious, the existential decision to work for the development of all is perfected by a decision to receive Communion daily, where this is possoble. By anyone given to theological reflection, daily Communion is seen to be the supreme evangelical counsel given (and not just offered) to all by Christ when He directed that, in His name, we should ask His Father: "Give us each day our daily bread" (Lk. 11, 3).[32]

Much more than are the three counsels recognized as such by Christian tradition, the evangelical counsel of daily Communion (which, anyhow, these other three promote) is capable of leading to the perfection of love, the soul of human development. It is the counsel of growth.

The existential choice in favor of the daily breaking of the Eucharistic Bread is a sacrificial choice. It leads to perfect abnegation, and therefore promotes that self-denial which conditions both personal and social development.

The Eucharistic Christ desires to be the daily bread of our love for one another, of our fraternal union, and therefore of our growth together for the lifting up of the world.

For the Catholic, therefore, the decision for development and the decision to receive Communion daily, involve one another.

It behoves us, for ourselves and for others, to make the sun of daily Communion shine forth as a value which affects the whole personality; as the most powerful factor for promoting the psychological, social, and ontological integration of the human personality; as, in a sense, a supreme value of this earthly life. We must do this, if we wish to help towards the efficacious and definitive crystalization of the redeemed human free will.

Is not daily Communion the best means to achieve the very purpose of our creation, the *raison d'être* of our earthly life—namely, the praise and service of Christ the Redeemer in the fulfillment of the twofold command of love?

If a man desires to love Jesus Christ above all things, can he reasonably deprive Christ of the opportunity to enter into him, and through him to glorify the Father and to serve His brethren? And this, day after day? On the other hand, would not the absence of a desire for daily Communion be the sign that some created being, and especially the "self," is loved more than Jesus?

The free, definitive, constantly renewed decision to receive Communion daily in order to increase in oneself the love of God and the love of the neighbor for God's sake, is, on the contrary, the existential decision *par excellence* whose dynamism entails a multiplicity of successive decisions to promote human development, even in its earthly aspects.

A means of socio-ecclesial integration, daily Communion is also a factor promoting the psychological and ontological integration of the human and Christian personality.

Modern man often feels cut away from his past and threatened by his future. The remedy which the Eucharist brings to this ever recurrent disintegration resulting from the human condition, has been admirably analyzed by Pope Pius XII:

> For many, the present is simply the wild rush of a torrent which sweeps men, like so much detritus, into the dark night of a future in which they will lose themselves with the very current that carries them along.
>
> Only the Church can lead men back from that darkness to the light; only the Church can give them awareness of a vigorous past, mastery of the present, confidence in the future. . . .
>
> On our countless altars, do we not daily see Christ, the divine Victim, whom arms reach out from end to end of the world, to enfold and embrace, at once in its past, in its present and in its future, the whole of human society? . . .
>
> In the holy Mass, men come to a greater awareness of their sinful past, and at the same time gain the immense blessings received in this memorial of Calvary—this memorial of the most sublime event in the history of mankind. They can receive the strength needed to free themselves from the deepest misery of the present, the misery of daily sins, and this to such an extent that even the most hardened feel the breath of the personal love of the God of Mercy. Their eyes are lifted towards a secure future, towards the consummation of time in the victory of the Lord, who is there on the altar; the victory of that Judge who one day will pronounce the final and definitive sentence. . . .
>
> In the holy Mass, therefore, the Church makes its greatest contributions to the building of human Society.[33]

Through the communicants, the Eucharistic Christ is the leaven in the dough of human society. By immersing them daily in the eternity of Christ, the daily Communion of these communicants saves their past, become a meritorious source of eternal life; helps them to become, at the cost of their own self-sacrifices, "the slaves of all" (cf. Mt. 10, 44) and the servants of the growth of the world; and even assures, as much as this is possible to the unstable free will of men, their final perseverance in divine love. Alienated as we partly are from our past and our future, it in some sort restores past and present to us, and in this way likens us to God with whom there is neither past nor future.[34] It divinizes both the temporal and the social structure of the created mind.

In these conditions, one understands why the Church, precisely because she is aware that "human fulfillment" constitutes, as it were, "a summary of our duties" (PP, 16), invites her children to eat daily the fruit of the Tree of Life at her "marriage supper of the Lamb," at the nuptial and sacrificial feast of the Mass (cf. Rev. 19, 9; 22, 2). The Church invites us to divinize, daily and with growing intensity, our imaginations, our sensibilities, our intellects, and our free wills through intimate contact with the human imagination, sensibility, intellect, and free will of Christ the Redeemer. In a sense, it can be said that the whole apostolic pedagogy of the Church and that of its most living members, are methodically directed towards securing a free, deliberate, personal, definitive, and increasingly deepened resolution to work, through and thanks to daily Communion, for the global development, human and supernatural, of all men.

To the technicians and the builders of the earthly city, the Church says: "It is neither daily Mass nor daily Communion that deflects you from your work or from your studies; in fact, the contrary is true. There can be no serious and sustained work without mortification of the passions, of the imagination, and of the sensual appetites; there can be no mortification of the lower psyche without frequent participation, through the Eucharist, in the death of Christ. If every day you receive Him who is eternal Light and eternal Wisdom, Him who is the Lord of the world and even of His enemies, Him who is the supreme author of the organic growth of mankind, you will gain a greater understanding and mastery of the earth in the service of man."

The decision to participate sacramentally and daily in the redemptive death of Christ, may be considered to be the "existential major decision" which gives meaning and supernatural efficacy to all the "minor decisions" to promote human development, while at the same time it anticipates and prepares for the supreme decision concerning coredemptive death.[35]

Is it not because this Eucharistic decision is constantly taken and renewed throughout the whole world by countless men and women, that the Church, as Vatican II says, continually grows in faith, in hope, and in charity?

Should it not also be said that, at least indirectly, this decision is the source of that progress of human history which the Providence of Christ, Creator and Redeemer, links organically with the progress of His Church?

To those who fail to see this relative progress, through fixing their eyes on the partial and periodic regressions which they witness, we answer with Paul VI:

> It may be that these persons are not realistic enough, and that they have not perceived the dynamism of a world which desires to live more fraternally—a world which, in spite of its ignorance, its mistakes, and even its sins, its relapses into barbarism, and its wanderings far from the road of salvation, is, even unaware, taking slow but sure steps towards its Creator. . . . Civilizations are born, develop, and die. But humanity is advancing along the path of history like the waves of a rising tide encroaching gradually on the shore.[36]

For the believer, there can be no doubt about the connection, on the one hand, between this "rising tide" and this dynamism of human history, and, on the other, the active and frequent participation in the Eucharistic sacrifice. One must, of course, distinguish the different levels of the growth of the world, but one cannot separate them, or ignore the influence of the Eucharist on the concrete unfolding of human history.[37]

The connection between the growth of the Church and the decision concerning Eucharistic development is more obvious. Through the Eucharist, the Good News, the Gospel, of which the Eucharist as we have seen is the summary and the synthesis, bears fruit and is developed throughout the whole world (cf. Col. 1, 6); thanks to the Eucharist, numerous Christians are "bearing fruit in every good work and increasing in the knowledge of God" (Col. 1, 10); because they more frequently and more fervently eat the Body of Christ, they increasingly attach themselves "to the Head, from whom the whole body, *nourished* and knit together through its joints and ligaments, *grows* with a growth that is from God" (Col. 2, 19). Thanks to the Eucharistic growth of the grain of mustard seed of the Church in its beginning, the "smallest of all seeds . . . becomes a tree, so that the birds of the air"—i.e. the nations—"come and make nests in its branches" (Mt. 13, 31-32; Ez. 17, 23; Deut. 4, 9-18). Christ, received frequently in the Eucharist, enfolds in His arms, through His Church, the whole of human history.

The adult Christian's decision to seek development through the Eucharist, enables the Church to fulfill the ancient command: "Increase and multiply, and fill the earth, and subdue it" (Gn. 1, 28), which command Christ came, not to abolish, but to fulfill in a new command: "Fill all things . . . that God may be everything to every one" (Eph. 4, 10; 1 Cor. 15, 27-28).[38] This decision is the seed sown in good soil: it brings forth "grain, growing up and increasing and yielding . . . a hundredfold" (Mk. 4, 8). It is the principal factor of the "Eucharistic pleromization of the world" through which the Church is constantly and increasingly filled with Christ, "the fullness of him who fills all in all" (Eph. 1, 23).[39]

The decision to receive Communion daily, a decision taken as a means to promote the self-development of others,[40] amounts almost to entry into a state of life; it is, in a sense, a public profession of the desire for the perfection of love. In this respect, it constitutes a voluntary setting apart[41] in the midst of the People of God and for that people, a development of the consecration inaugurated by baptism. It is the Christian's response to the prayer that Christ offered for him to the Father: "And for their sake I consecrate myself, that they may be consecrated in truth" (Jn. 17, 19)—that is, that they may agree to share in my own consecration.

Jesus is He whom the Father has marked with His seal—that is, with His Spirit; and whom He has consecrated and sent into the world in order that He might consecrate Himself, as "the first-born of all creation," under the breath of this same Spirit.[42] Human development is the fruit of His consecrating sacrifice. The initial consecration of Christ, the Anointed of the Spirit, is orientated towards the sacrifice,[43] polarized by the final consecration of the world, of all mankind. John the Baptist had to decrease in order that Jesus might increase (Jn. 3, 30) to the sacrifice of Himself for the growth of the Church and of the world. Jesus is the bloody Victim for our development. The Lamb of God died in order that we might also agree to be victims for the lifting up of the world. There can be no development, no growth, without sacrifice and without abnegation. The consecration received by the Christian in baptism and confirmation, orientates him towards the sacrifices demanded for personal and social development, just as Christ's consecration by His Father, in the Spirit, orientated Him towards His paschal sacrifice and towards the return to the Father, a return in which He incorporates the fruits of His kenosis.[44]

In the final analysis, does not development mean the building up by all men of good will, in union with Christ, of that perfect Man grown to full age in whom is realized the fullness of Christ—i.e. the Church, the Whole Christ, this Church which, in a sense, includes the cosmos and, *a fortiori*, the natural order of human growth in its totality?[45] But can one separate from his paschal inclusion of human growth in the development towards the pleroma, the no less paschal decrease to which Saint John the Baptist referred: "He must increase, but I must decrease" (Jn. 3, 30)? Is not human development secured by the simultaneous operation of a certain law of decrease (of the old man) and of the natural and supernatural law of increase of the new man? In order that Christ may grow, we must, in various and complementary respects, decrease and increase. The decision to receive Communion daily is therefore a coredemptive decision which brings both these laws into play, provided that it is regarded and lived as something which raises and divinizes a man's professional and social life.[46]

This decision is therefore the choice of a coredemptive existence which inserts into the Eucharistic Sacrifice the development which it stimulates. It manifests and intensifies the will to share in the sacrifice of the Lamb of God for the consecration of the world. It is already a sacrificial consecration to the development of the Church and of the world.

*   *   *   *   *

Thanks be to you, Eucharistic heart of Jesus, for having willed to place Yourself at the head of a world in growth and in development, through the sacrifice of Your Pasch.

Praise be to You for ceaselessly immolating Yourself and for offering at every moment Your flesh for the life of the world (cf. Jn. 6, 51).

You are the living Bread that came down from Heaven that we might eat It and never die (cf. Jn. 6, 50). In receiving Your testimony and Your Eucharistic offering, we bear witness "that God is true" (cf. Jn. 3, 33).

We offer and consecrate ourselves as victims to Your hunger and Your thirst to grow in us and in all mankind.

To You, creative and redemptive Bread, we give completely our being, our freedom, our work, our whole activity.

Come within us, as the Expiator of capitalist greed and Marxist atheism, as the Repairer of our selfishness.

Be to us the daily Bread of our growth together. Come, Son of Man, to work within us, not for the food that perishes, but in order to satisfy fully the hunger of men with an eternal food which You freely give to us. For it is You that the Father has marked with His seal, the Holy Spirit (cf. Jn. 6, 27).

Lamb of God, You have come from the Father into the world: through us, take now this world into Your Heart which enfolds it and which is towards the Father's bosom (Jn. 1, 18).[47]

Appendix: The Significance and the Limits of the Evangelical Counsel of Daily Communion

Certain readers may be surprised to read in this final chapter: "Daily Communion is the most powerful factor of the social, psychological, and ontological integration of the human person."

I do not mean, however, any and every type of daily Communion; for example, of the daily Communion received hastily and casually, without deep respect; or of the type where the communicant is indulging in a kind of spiritual egoism, having a *tête-à-tête* with Jesus in the Host, while ignoring the "horizontal" consequences which daily Communion ought to entail.

Nor am I unaware of the very real danger that the quality of a Christian life might come to be reckoned by the number of Communions, without any thought for the necessary awareness, the preparation, and thanksgiving (normally of fifteen minutes duration for an adult).

I am also aware of the norms laid down by the moralists when they were commenting on the decisions of Saint Pius X; for example, here is what Cappello wrote:

"The confessor should refuse permission for frequent Communion to those who habitually omit a serious preparation and a suitable thanksgiving, in accordance with the strength, conditions, and duties of each person; because they show that they do not approach the sacred Table with due deliberation and that therefore they lack the proper dispositions. . . . The faithful who desire to communicate frequently should seek the judgment or advice of the confessor, who, in this domain, holds a declarative and non-imperative authority. The confessor may, *per accidens*, forbid frequent Communion if it cannot be practiced without detriment to the duties of the penitent's state in life" (*De Sacramentis*, Rome, 1928, t.I., par. 511-512).

But in our day, when religious sociologists are everywhere noting the drop in frequent Communion, I wanted to show the meaning of this evangelical counsel in the twofold history, temporal and salvific, of the human race.

NOTES TO CHAPTER THREE

1. "Unaided" must be read here as referring to the absence of aid from social influences, as the context clearly shows. There is, of course, no suggestion of the absence of divine aid.

2. Paul VI, *Populorum Progressio,* par. 15 (C.T.S. translation). Further reference to this encyclical in the notes will appear as PP.

3. PP, par. 42, quoting *Pensées,* no. 434, ed. Brunschvicg.

4. PP, 15. Cf. Mt. 25, 14-20.

5. PP, 15. This paragraph, stressing the responsibility of each man for his own destiny, for his success or his failure, even in an underdeveloped milieu, might seem to contradict what is said in par 6: ". . . to seek to do more, know more, and have more, in order to be more: that is what men aspire to now when a greater number of them are condemned to live in conditions that make this lawful desire illusory." There is certainly an element of tension between these two paragraphs, but not of contradiction. Paragraph 6 does not say that no progress is possible for the majority of men who live in the underdeveloped countries. It merely says that *all* the types of lawful progress which they could desire are, in the present circumstances, impossible for them. Furthermore, there is always a supernatural level of development which is largely independent of the natural level.

6. PP, 42.

7. PP, 20, citing Maritain.

8. PP, 16.

9. PP, 19; cf. 18.

10. Cf. PP, 24.

11. PP, 6; cf. note 5.

12. PP, par. 21.

13. PP, par. 6.

14. PP, par. 13.

15. PP, par. 28.

16. Our doing so can be justified: on the one hand, it is in line with the profound sense envisaged by Saint Luke, for whom the history of the Church which he gives us is, in a sense, a prophecy and a paradigm; on the other, it is in line with the interpretation of the New Testament presupposed, at least implicitly, by LG, 65; cf. the following note.

17. LG, 65. In his " 'Credo' of the People of God," Paul VI explains the precise meaning of this progress of the Church: "The true growth of the Kingdom of God cannot be measured by the progress of civilization, of science or of technology: it consists in an ever deepening knowledge of the unfathomable riches of Christ, in ever stronger hope in eternal blessings, in an ever more fervent response to the love of God, and in an ever more generous acceptance of grace and holiness by men" (C.T.S. translation, pp. 13-14).

18. GS, 39. 2.

19. Saint Irenaeus's image: *Adv. Haer.* IV. 20. 1 (MG, 7, 1032).

20. PP, 15.

21. Cf. Rom. 8, 21; cf. B. de Margerie S.J., *R. Niebuhr, théologien de la communauté mondiale,* Desclée de Brouwer, Bruges, 1969, Part 3, Chap. II, par. 1, 2.

22. PP, 79.

23. This is the interpretation of this verse in the Jerusalem Bible. It is in full conformity with Eph. 1, 13-14; 4, 30; 2 Cor. 1, 22.

24. Cf, Chapter One, C.

25. Cf. Jn. 8, 44. 45.

26. Cf. Chapter One, note 11.

27. PP, 16.

28. The final sentence of the text to which note 2 of our Chapter Five refers. Bultmann also says there that "Jesus expresses no conception of a human ideal, no thought of a development of human capacities"; but how would he interpret the parable of the talents (Mt. 25, 14-30) and other Gospel texts?

29. PP, 47.

30. *Ibid.*

31. The *temporal efficacy* of our engagement, we say here: what we mean is that *(other things being equal, however)* he who receives the Eucharist can efficaciously deploy his qualities and natural virtues more readily than others can do.

Cf. the text of Pius XII and that of John XXIII cited in note 37; see also B. de Margerie S.J., *A Igreja em estado de diálogo,* Manhumirim, Brazil, 1965, pp. 303-353.

32. In the light of Jn. 14, 13; 16, 23-27, it is clear that the Christian recites the "Our Father" in the name of Jesus and in union with Him. Besides, the patristic and ecclesiastical tradition has rightly interpreted the request for daily bread in a Eucharistic manner; see the decree *Sacra Tridentina Synodus,* approved by Pius X, 20 December 1905 (*Actes de saint Pie X,* Paris, Bonne Presse, t. II, pp. 252-253). We have dealt fully with this subject in an article, "Rythme eucharistique et pastorale contemporaine," *Rev. Eucharistique du Clergé* (Montreal), 69 (1966), 257-278. We have there attempted to suggest how to present at the present time the evangelical counsel of daily Communion, against the wiles of the prince of the world. Here, within the framework of a fresh presentation, we take up again in part some of the ideas dealt with there.

33. Pius XII, allocution, "La Elevatezza" of 20 February 1945; AAS, 38 (1946), 150-151.

34. Cf. Saint Thomas Aquinas, *Commentaries on the Sentences,* 1 *Sent.* 8. 1. 1.

35. Cf. our Chapter Five, sub fine.

36. PP, 79 and 17.

37. Cf. John XXIII, citing Pius XII, in 1960: AAS, 52 (1960), 402: "The Eucharist is a mystery of physical life: directly, of eternal physical life, because, as Jesus assures us, those who receive It with proper dispositions are certain to have a glorious resurrection on the last day; indirectly, of temporal physical life, because, in developing the Christian life and good moral behavior, It preserves the recipients from the many infirmities which contaminate the body and torment sinful life" (cf. note 31).

38. Cf. L. Ligier S.J., *Péché d'Adam et Péché du Monde,* Paris, 1961, t. II, p. 342: the author here shows how Saint Paul, in the Epistles of the Captivity, has paraphrased Gn. 1, 28 (*ibid.,* note 81)—a text of Gn. cited by PP, 22.

39. Cf. Chapter Four, note 135; Chapter Thirteen, note 14.

40. Cf. PP, 34: "Man is truly man in as far as, master of his own acts and judge of their worth, he is author of his own advancement, in keeping with the nature which was given to him by his Creator, and whose possibilities and exigencies he himself freely assumes." One cannot "develop" others, but one can and should help them to develop themselves. The concept of development is inseparable from that of responsibility.

41. "Set apart," that is, *de facto,* not *de jure:* this counsel of daily Communion is offered to all, given to all, but accepted and practiced only by a minority. We speak here of "the desire for the perfection of love" and not necessarily of the

subjectively efficacious tendency towards it; because the decree, *Sancta Tridentina Synodus,* already cited, has reminded us that to receive Communion it is not indispensable (however highly desirable) to be free from all deliberate venial sin. We say that the habit of daily Communion constitutes almost a state of life, because "the fruits of daily Communion are incomparably more abundant than those of weekly or monthly Communion" (*ibid.;* see my article, already cited, pp. 260-261). Now, the decision concerning daily Communion is the choice to seek assured continuity of spiritual progress, and, in this respect, can be regarded as, in a sense, the entry into a state of life—one which would be no other than that to which the baptized person aspires in virtue of the very dynamism of the baptismal grace, completely polarized by the Eucharist. The Eucharist is the sacrament which produces, *ex opere operato,* the perfection of love, fundamental law of Christian action. The remission of venial sins is one of the special fruits of the Eucharist, sacrament of the fervor of love. Daily Communion does not presuppose perfect holiness, since Its purpose is to confer this on him who places no obstacle in its way. "Because you are constantly sinning, receive Communion constantly," Saint Ambrose says in substance (*De Sacramentis* IV, 6, par. 28).

42. Cf. Jn. 10, 36; Col. 1, 15; Lk. 4, 1.

43. Westcott, cited by R. E. Brown S.S. (*The Gospel according to John,* Anchor Bible, N.Y. 1966, p. 261), thus interprets Jn. 6, 27 in the light of 10, 36: "consecration to sacrifice."

44. Cf. this very beautiful text of Gerson: "Exivit (Christus) secundum animam per creationis emanationem et ad Deum vadit per sui et aliorum omnium in Deum revolutionem intelligibilem; et sicut omnia quodammodo a Deo accepit in sua creatione dum propter eam facta sunt omnia, sic omnia refert in Deum dilective proportionnaliter satis ad primum exitum et reditum aeternalem" (Sermon *A Deo exivit,* edited by A. Combes, *Essai sur la critique de Ruysbroeck par Gerson,* Paris, 1945, t. I, p. 648).

45. Cf. the interpretation of Saint Paul by Father Benoit, Chapter Four, note 135.

46. Cf. John XXIII, in *Pacem in Terris:* "It is necessary that human beings, in the intimacy of their own consciences, should so live and act in their temporal lives as to create a synthesis between scientific, technical, and professional elements on the one hand, and spiritual values on the other" (C.T.S. translation, p. 54). It is precisely for this purpose that we end this book on Christology with an invitation to Christian and human action. Contemplative reflection should issue in action which transforms the world. This is also the undoubted aim of Paul VI in PP, about which one could read

P. E. Charbonneau, *Desenvolvimento dos Povos,* Herder, S. Paulo (Brazil), 1967 (303 pages).

47. We are adopting the translation of Jn. 1, 18 given by I. de la Potterie in *Biblica,* 43 (1962), 379-387.

BIBLIOGRAPHY

A. D'ADHEMAR, S.J., *De Verbo Incarnato*, Paris, 1930.

E. B. ALLO, O.P., *L'Apocalypse*, Paris, 1921.

ST. AUGUSTIN, *de Trinitate*, Bibliothèque Augustinienne, Paris, 1955.

— *in Joannem* (M. L. 35).

H. DE BARENTON, O.F.M.CAP., *La dévotion au Sacré-Coeur*, Paris, 1914.

ST. R. BELLARMIN, S.J., *Controversia de Summo Pontifice*, Vivès, Paris, 1870.

— *Opera oratoria posthuma*, Rome, 1940, *sq*, 9 vol.

P. BENOIT, O.P., *Exégèse et Théologie*, Paris, 1961, 2 vol.

D. BONHOEFFER., *Résistance et Soumission*, Genève, 1967.

— *Christology*, London, 1966.

F. BONNEFOY, O.F.M., *Primauté du Christ selon l'Ecriture et la Tradition*, Herder, Rome, 1959.

H. BOUESSE, O.P., *Le Sauveur de Monde*, t. I, Place du Christ, Chambéry, 1951.

H. BOUILLARD, S.J., *Logique de la foi*, Paris, 1964.

L. BOUYER., *Les deux économies du gouvernement divin, Initiation Théologique* t. II, Paris, 1952.

G. DE BROGLIE, S.J., *Le principe fondamental de la Mariologie, Maria*, t. VI, Paris, 1961.

R. BROWN, S.S., *The Gospel according to John*, N.Y., 1966.

R. BULTMANN, *Jésus Christ and Mythology*, N.Y., 1958.

STE. CATHERINE DE SIENNE, *Dialogue*, éd. Hurtaud, Paris, 1913.

L. CERFAUX, *Le Christ dans la théologie de Saint Paul*, Paris, 1954.

Collectiff, *La Collégialité épiscopale*, Paris, 1965.

Collectif, *La Parole de Dieu en Jésus-Christ*, Castermann, Tournai, 1961.

118

Collectif, *Cor Jesu,* ouvrage dirigé par A. BEA, S.J., Rome, 1959, 2 vols.

J. COLSON, *Episcopat catholique : collégialité et primauté,* Paris, 1963.

J. COMBLIN, *Le Christ dans l'Apocalypse,* Paris, 1965.

Concile Oécuménique Vatican II; Constitutions, décrets, déclarations. Ed. Bilingue, Centurion, Paris, 1967.

Y. M. J. CONGAR, O.P., *Mystère du Temple,* Paris, 1958.

— *Voies du Dieu vivant,* Paris, 1962.

— *Esquisse du Mystère de l'Eglise,* Paris, 1953.

— *Jésus-Christ,* Paris. 1966.

— *Sainte Eglise,* Paris, 1963.

— *Episcopat et Eglise universelle,* Paris, 1962.

G. CRES-Y, *De la Science à la Théologie,* Paris-Neuchatel, 1965.

O. CULLMANN, *Christology of the New Testament,* London, 1959.

J. DANIELOU, S.J., *Message évangélique et culture hellénistique,* Paris, 1961.

— *Théologie du Judéo-Christianisme,* Tournai, 1961.

— *Essai sur le mystère de l'Histoire,* Paris, 1953.

J. M. DUFORT, S.J., *Récapitulation paulinienne dans l'exégèse des Pères,* Sciences Ecclésiastiques, 12 (1960) 21-38.

F. X. DURRWELL, C.SS.R., *La Résurrection de Jésus, Mystère du salut,* Paris, 1961.

A. FEUILLET, *Le Christ Sagesse de Dieu,* Paris, 1966.

J. DE FINANCE, S.J., *Connaissance de l'Etre,* Paris, 1966.

H. FRIES, *Encyclopédie de la foi,* 4 vol., Paris, 1967.

J. GALOT, *Rédemption, Mystère d'Alliance,* Bruges, 1965.

GIRAUD, *De l'Union à Notre Seigneur dans sa vie de victime,* Paris, 1932.

J. D. GODSEY, *Theology of Dietrich Bonhoeffer,* London, 1963.

Gott in Welt, (Festgabe fuer K. Rahner) Freiburg, 1958.

P. HARTMANN, S.C.J., *Le sens plénier de la réparation du péché,* Louvain, 1955.

HOUSSIAU, *Christologie d'Irénée,* Louvain, 1955.

ST. IRENEE, *Adversus Haereses.*

C. JOURNET, CARDINAL, *l'Eglise du Verbe Incarné,* Bruges, 1951.

B. KLOPPENBURG, O.F.M., *O espiritismo no Brasil,* Petropolis, 1964.

M. J. LAGRANGE, O.P., *Evangile selon Saint Jean,* Paris, 1948.

LAMARCHE, *Le Christ vivant,* Paris, 1966.

M. DE LA TAILLE, S.J., *Mysterium Fidei,* Paris, 1924.

R. LATOURELLE, S.J., *Théologie de la Révélation,* Bruges, 1966.

J. LAWSON, *Biblical theology of Irenaeus,* London, 1948.

J. LEBRETON, S.J., *Origine du dogme de la Trinité,* Paris, 1919.

J. LECUYER, C.S.SP., *Le sacrifice de la Nouvelle Alliance,* Lyon, 1962.

B. LEEMING, S.J., *Adnotationes de Verbo Incarnato,* Rome, 1936.

L. LIGIER, S.J., *Péché d'Adam et Péche du Monde,* Paris, 1961, 2 vol.

B. LONERGAN, S.J., *De Verbo Incarnato*, Rome, 1964.
E. LONGPRE, O.F.M., *Eucharistie et expérience mystique, DSAM,*
    t. IV, Paris, 1961.
H. DE LUBAC, S.J., *La prière du P. Tielhard*, Paris, 1964.
— *Blondel et Teilhard de Chardin*, Paris, 1965.
— *Teilhard, Missionnaire et Apologiste*, Toulouse, 1966.
B. DE MARGERIE, S.J., R. NIEBUHR, *théologien de la communauté
    mondiale*, Paris-Brussels, 1969.
— *Le Coeur de Marie, Coeur de l'Eglise*, Paris, 1967.
— *A Igreja em estado de dialogo*, Manhumirim, Brazil, 1965.
— *Padres Profetas e Mistagogos*, S. Paulo, 1968.
STE. MARGUERITE-MARIE ALACOQUE, *Vie et Oeuvre*, éd. Gauthey,
    Paris, 1915.
J. MARITAIN, *De la grace et de l'humanité de Jésus*, Bruges, 1967.
— *Le paysan de la Garonne*, Paris, 1966.
R. MARLE, S.J., *Bultmann et l'interprétation du Nouveau Testa-
    ment*, Paris, 1966.
— *D. Bonhoeffer, témoin de Jésus-Christ parmi ses frères*,
    Tournai, 1967.
E. MASCALL, *Christ, the Christian and the Church*, London, 1946.
CH. MASSABKI, DOM, O.S.B., *Le Christ rencontre de deux amours*,
    Paris, 1962.
R. C. McCREARY, O.F.M. CAP., *Christ the Savior according to St.
    Lawrence of Brindisi*, Laurentianum 4 (1963) 401-430.
— *The Redemptive Incarnation according to St. Lawrence
    of Brindisi*, Laurentianum 6 (1965) 315-328.
— *The glorification of Christ in the Thought of St Lawrence*,
    Laurentianum 10 (1969) 401-412.
E. MERSCH, S.J., *Théologie du Corps Mystique*, Paris-Bruxelles,
    1944.
— *Le Corps Mystique du Christ*, Louvain, 1933.
J. B. METZ, *Christliche Anthropozentrik*, Munich, 1962.
C. F. MOONEY, S.J., *Teilhard de Chardin et le Mystère du
    Christ*, Paris, 1968. (Original work published in English,
    N.Y., 1966).
H. MUHLEN, *Der Heilige Geist als Person*, Munster, 1967.
M. J. NICOLAS, O.P., *Théotokos*, Tournai, 1965.
P. NORTH, S.J., *Teilhard and the Creation of the Soul*, Mil-
    waukee, 1967.
M. PENIDO, TEIXEIRA-LEITE, *O mistério des Sacramentos*, Pe-
    tropolis, 1961.
PHILLIPPE DE LA TRINITE, O.C.D., *Rome et Teilhard*, Paris, 1964.
Problèmes actuels de christologie, ouvrage publié sous la di-
    rection de H. Bouessé, O.P., Paris, 1965.
K. RAHNER, S.J., *Ecrits Théologiques*, Bruges.
H. RAMIERE, S.J., *L'Apostolat de la Prière*, Toulouse, 9ᵉ éd.
E. RIDEAU, S.J., *La Pensée du P. Teilhard de Chardin*, Paris,
    1965.
L. SABOURIN, S.J., *Rédemption Sacrificielle*, Bruges, 1961.

M. J. SCHEEBEN, *Les Mystères du Christianisme*, Bruges, 1947.

E. SCHILLEBEECKX, O.P., *Marie, Mère de la Rédemption*, Paris. 1963.

— *Révélation et théologie*, Bruxelles, 1965.

R. SCHNACKENBURG, *Le Message moral du N.T.*, Lyon, 1963.

O. SEMMELROTH, S.J., *Maria, Urbild der Kirche*, Wurzburg, 1950.

P. SMULDERS, S.J., *La vision de Teilhard*, Paris, 1965.

P. TEILHARD DE CHARDIN, S.J., *Oeuvres*, Seuil, Paris, 9 vols.

G. THILS, *Propos et problèmes de la Théologie des religionsnon chrétiennes*, Bruxelles, 1965.

ST. THOMAS D'AQUIN, *Summa Theologiae*, Alba, Paulinae, Rome, 1962.

S. TROMP, S.J., *Corpus Christi quod est Ecclesia*, t. II., *de Christo Capite*, t. III., *de spiritu Christi anima*, Rome, 1960.

H. URS VON BALTHASAR, *Liturgie cosmique*, Paris, 1947.

G. WINGREN, *Man and the Incarnation*, A study in the biblical theology of Irenaeus, London, 1959.